THE 256 ODU OF IFA

CUBAN AND TRADITIONAL

VOL. 1

Eji Ogbe y Ogbe Oyeku

MARCELO MADAN

NOTE TO THIS EDITION

As we have already noticed in our previous Ifá literatures, it is about transcription of manuscript documents, many of them unpublished, with different wording and literary styles, I have always tried to keep in essence, the idea of what was wanted to express, for Therefore, it is quite difficult to achieve uniformity of style in this regard. In this new presentation I show in each of the Odu, everything from the literature of Afro-Cuban Ifá and traditional African Ifá.

It is in my interest, to provide Ifá students this time, a broad vision in all its dimensions of what Ifá can encompass, taking into account, in addition, that what is presented in this is not everything, because Ifá is much deeper. and his literary work is much more abundant than what I show here, this is only a part, even when I have added to these volumes' concepts from the previously published ifá treatises, as well as traditional ifá. In addition, it is not my intention here to suggest any kind of supremacy between the two trends, only to show them as each of them is presented and that it is the reader himself who judges and prefers its future use. My aim is to offer you the possibility of having at hand, a renewed tool for study, broader and more effective that allows you at the same time, to enter the learning of both literatures without limitations or discrimination, each one in its field, because ultimately, the knowledge of Ifá is universal and is for everyone alike.

GRATEFULNESS

Thanks to Olodumare, for having enlightened me and allow to create this work, to bc ablc to throw thc light of knowledge to everyone who needs it.

Thanks to Orunmila spirit of light that guides me and takes me along the right path.

Thanks to Obatala, my guard angel who always accompanies me and provides timely protection.

Thanks to my maternal grandmother and godmother Rosa Torrez (Shangó Womí)

Thanks to my godfather Rubén Pineda Baba Ejiogbe

CONTENT

Chapter

1.- BÀBÁ ÉJÌOGBÈ

+

I	I
I	I
I	I
I	I

I PRAY

Bàbá Éjìogbè ala lekun moni lekun okó Ajá lolá ọmọdú Aboşun Ọmọ e ní koşé idi kere şe ka mu ìleké Ọmọ lorí A dífá fún ala deşe imapapaporo timbà beledí agogo.

Iyere:

Eeşi ìrí máa (4 veces) Ikú furí bú jènià

1

Eeṣi ìrí máa (4 veces) Àrùn furí bú jènià

Eeṣi ìrí máa (4 veces) Ófò furí bú jènià

Eeṣi ìrí máa (4 veces) Ejo furí bú jènià

Eeṣi ìrí máa (4 veces) Iyan furí bú jènià

Eeṣi ìrí máa (4 veces) Ogu furí bú jènià

Òṣé mí ni òhen, Òṣé mí ni òhen, Òṣé mí ni òhen.....

IFA de

- Long-lived, living up to anxiety.
- Of wars.
- Of inconsideration.
- Of humility and patience.

PROVERBS:

- Never the way of Ikú is closed to the dog, just like the vulture in air
- The hole opens its mouth, the hole does not open its mouth for fun
- The Vulture perches on a body without life and says: I am on a corpse thanks to Éjìogbè
- The fish's tail does not stop moving
- The Elephant is very strong but not strong enough to defeat the wind.
- The eyes cannot go up from the head.

2

- The Okra cannot grow taller than the one that planted it. If it grows like this, we cut it down and pluck it up.
- No hat can be more famous than a crown.
- The head bears the body and a single king rules a people.
- Young feathers grow bushier than old ones.
- Dead king put king.
- I have everything and I lack everything
- It is a mistake not to learn from mistakes.
- When the head is on the shoulders, the thought on the horizon and the feet on the salty water, we have no doubt that we are facing the sea.
- While there is life, there is hope
- No sound is so loud that it can overshadow the sound of the bell.

BORN:

- Put a piece of Obí under the left foot of the person who is doing an ìtan.
- The ìtan of the saint.
- The government coup.
- That the Òsányin casserole for the saint does not have a candle because Bàbá took it away
- that the Awo who has this Odù de Ifá cannot kill animals for pleasure without first asking Òrúnmìlà.
- The dispersion of languages
- May the Awo of this Odù and Ogbè Ìròsùn never walk together

3

- That Olófin leave the Ifá room after his meal on the 6th day
- Awan fogẹdẹ
- The rivers
- That Òrúnmìlà only eat adie dúdú (black) by Olófin's sentence and he pass his hand with epo (palm oil) and adie fat so that he does not get Òfò
- Blood vessels and lymph
- Him because the saints are given water when they come, because they come thirsty (Olófin road and the children)
- He washes the legs of the feathered animals that are sacrificed to the saints and Òrìṣà.

BRAND

- Mitral valve problems
- Humility and patience

SIGNALIZE

- A lot of willpower to be able to win.
- War and persecution.
- Treason.
- Here the person gets tired of continuing to carry an acquired responsibility on their shoulders.
- That stubbornness, the cult of personality, women and money lose the person and can take him before the law to be convicted.
- Sacrifice of love for the beloved woman, but it is badly

reciprocated.

- That the person has nowhere to live.

IFÁ SAYS

- The spine and sternum, support of the rib cage
- The will
- Of losses and tears
- Of three brothers, one Ọmọ Òrúnmìlà, another Ọmọ from Ọbàtàlá and the other from Yémọjá
- Of masks and blinds
- From the sea level and its dire consequences
- The hunter who had a bad situation and Ifá advised him to do orugbo with a holster and arrows
- The Butterfly that burned its wings for wanting to fly before its time
- From the Ekutele's war with Òṣùn, Ògún and Òṣósii, where Òṣósii catches him, Òṣùn sentences him and Ògún kills him.

PROHIBITIONS

- When you see this Ifá, you have to spend seven days without going outside.
- You can't wear striped clothes because you are attracted to prison.
- Don't get into anything you don't care about.
- Do not receive or carry messages at night.

- Do not enter any house without permission to avoid a hot flash.
- Do not allow children to crawl on the floor in your home
- You can't play interest so you don't lose.
- You cannot play or be a player because you are going to destruction and ruin
- You cannot have three women at the same time 1, 2 or 4
- Éjìogbè's spouse must be of a different color from his white or black, never half-blood
- You never go around with witchcraft things.
- You do not eat Sweet Potato, eggs or Soursop.

RECOMMENDATIONS

- Feed your head
- Must live organized in every way

EWÉ OF ÉJÌOGBÈ

Mangle rojo	Palo Bobo	Mano pilón	Itamorreal	Ceiba
Orquidi Ayúa	Bejuco Bi	Guira	Cundiamor	Coralillo
Orozun Iroko	Rosa cimarrona	Jobo	Romerillo	Almácigo
Granada	Algodón	Pródigiosa	Piñón de Rosa	Atiponlá
Bleo Blanco	Almendra	Canutillo		

For more information see: Encyclopedia of Ifá herbs by Marcelo Madan

PÀTAKI LISTING

1. When Olófin invited the 16 méjì

WORKS WITH ÉJÌOGBÈ

Ẹbọ for Ikú unló

A rotten animal found dead in the street, which is put into a basket. The interested party is made sarayeye with adié funfun and jujú is added to the basket, the two adie funfun are given to Odùdúwà, the basket is placed in the doorway of the house on the days that Ifá says.

Ẹbọ Intorí Àrùn

Lerí de Àgbò, igba with añarí Òrun, adié, whatever clothes

are on, eku, eja, the person is undressed and añarí is thrown over them so that it runs through their body, is picked up and goes to the Ẹbọ

Ẹbọ For the Awo Bàbá Éjìogbè:

Àkúko, Ẹtù, Ẹiyelé, three different Igi, a ẹyin adié, a ẹyin from ẹtù, a ẹyin from Ẹiyelé, jujú méta from each of these birds, Àṣo ara, gbogbo Àṣe, ọpọlọpọ owó.

Ẹbọ to refresh the Ọṣẹ

Àkúko, adié méjì, Ọṣẹ méta, awan (basket), Ẹtù méta, eku, eja, epo, ọpọlọpọ owó

Sarayeye to the interested party with Àkúko and the adié and they are given to Èṣù and Òrúnmìlà. The Ọṣẹ (soap) are loaded with the eyebale of Èṣù and Òrúnmìlà so that the person concerned can bathe with them. The umbebolo basket. The Ẹtù méta are buried in the courtyard of the house

Ẹbọ to keep business

Àkúko méta, land of the corners of the business, atitan bata, Àṣo, ataare, eku, epo, ọ pọ lọ pọ owó, after fact the Ẹbọ is given one of the Àkúko to Elégbà, one to Èṣù in the corner and one to Èṣù in Ṣilikún ilé.

9

For this Ifá take hold of Èṣù and Òrúnmìlà, so you have to do three Ẹbọ on the same day, on the way to Èṣù and Ideu. Rides on an Iṣé de Òsányin (osanyin)

First ẹbọ

Osaidie fifeṣu, a güiro, eku, eja, epo, eja tútù méta, èbìtì, obe, dirt from a road and other ingredients, opolopo owó, take it to a road and put it next to an old house, return to the Awo's house, greet Elégbà, drink water and rest for a while.

Second ẹbọ

A gio-gio, an igbon (jug) with Omí, an eleguede, aṣọ ará, land of a road, atitan ilè, atitan bata, eku, eja, epó. Take him to the same place as the previous one, return to the awo's house, greet Elégbà, drink some water and rest for a while.

Third ẹbọ.

An Aunko kéke, an adié, aṣọ aperi, a fryer (small clay pot), a güiro, 16 Ẹiyelé funfun, 16 meters of aṣọ funfun, eku, eja, epo. Take to the same place as the previous ones and then return home.

NOTE:

When Bábà Éjìogbè does not take ẹbọ, an eel is placed inside a basin with water, Òbàtála is presented with Ẹiyelé méta funfun and he kneels before Bábà until the eel dies, then the

10

eel is taken, opened and They give the three Ẹiyelé, the lerí, elese and okàn méta of the Ẹiyelé are made with iye and are linked with seeds of eleguede, ewé bleo blanco, orí, efún, pray in atepon Ifá for this Odù and mount on an Iṣé de Òsányin(osanyin).

Work to advance in government or work

A cotton tower is made, inside the generals of those who have to do with the matter of promotion are placed, oyin and efún are added, two ìtanná are smeared in oyin and iyobo funfun and Òbàtála is lit next to the tower from Thursday to Thursday Before going to that place, 8 ebomisí will be given with Ewé: Poppy and 8 with White Bell and every time you go to that place, iye of Ewé: Poppy, jujú ashes from ẹiyelé funfun will be smeared on the face , every time the ìtanná is finished, they are renewed on Thursdays. When the promotion is achieved, it will be fulfilled with Òbàtála A lamp is lit for Òbàtála for umbo Ilè in a funfun dish with ẹyin ẹiyelé, almond oil, orí, name and surnames. For this ifá the awó must always have Òpèle in his pocket.

For Òsóìbò Ikú: aṣinimá is made with ẹiyelé okàn funfun, the ẹiyelé is given to the powder of the pomegranate with charcoal.

By intori Àrùn

He is given Ẹiyelé behind Elégbà. Indicates mitral valve

11

problems-

To remove Ogu from the stomach

take infusion of rose apple root, pionia root and sea fan.

So that the Awo can speak Ifá

An Işé de Òsányin is prepared with silver dime coins.

<u>To solve situations</u>

Lerí de eku, de eja tútù, obí kola, obí motyiwao.

To solve situations or difficulties with women

Òrúnmìlà is given a smoked Jutía tied around the waist with a flag necklace and Òrúnmìlà is given two adié dudu.

<u>work for impotence</u>

Two door frame inşerí (nails) are taken and cut to the size of the penis, washed with ewé guengueré omiero, then eaten as a salad. ẹbọ tentiboru (ẹbọ of the Odù) is made and then one of the inşerí is placed as a reinforcement of Ògún and another inside his Ifá.

<u>Work to avoid problems with the godson</u>

Take an Àkúko funfun, clean it with it, open its chest with the obe of the pine forest and load it with an ocha snail washed with Elégbà, a piece of paper with the generals and the Odu of the godson and Bábà Éjìogbè, put on the ará of the Àkúko in front of Elégbà and at night it is taken to be buried on the seashore and it is said: when this Àkúko manages to get out of the joro-joro by himself then the friendship with my godson will be broken.

To beat the Arayes

Three long-necked gourds are taken, Almagre is poured into one, efun into another and ifá charcoal iyé into the third. They are passed through the board and iyefá is thrown, they are tied with three threads and three adié are given, a pupa to the Almagre, a funfun to the efun and a dudu to the one that contains Òsányin charcoal iyé, then the three güiros are placed to Elegba.

Work to raise health

With iré aṣegun ota or iré ayé, please lerí with: ẹtu méjì, a funfun and a jabada, if the person is ọmọ from Ṣàngó, kobori aparó méjì and let the eyebale fall on Ṣàngó.

Work for Éjìogbè

In a small wooden box you put a small jar with water and sand from the river and another with water and sand from the sea, apart from it you put efun, orí, eku, eja, àgbado,, to this you give Ẹiyelé mérin funfun and the lerí they are thrown into the box and two obí painted with efun are

13

placed on the lid and the box is placed under the interested party's bed, at the end of the year of having done the work, the obí are scraped in the street, they fill the pots with their corresponding water, the inside is given Ẹiyelé mérin funfun again and it is sealed again after adding the corresponding lerí works, the box is closed and two new obí painted with funfun are placed on top of it and puts it back under the bed at the head of the interested party.

Work for Elégbà to work

Take an igba with water, chop 16 very fine ilè and pour iyefá on it, stir it with the tip of the irofá praying Bábà Éjìogbè and pour over Elégbàra.

Iṣé Òsányin to go umbo (luck)

A silver step, akokàn from ẹtu, inso from Ewúre, atare, iyefá, obí motiguao, obí kolá, anun, aira, eku, oti, oñi, before closing it, omí abaró is added, it is covered in inso from Ekùn, it lives behind of Òrúnmìlà.

To get lucky

ẹbọ is made with: Abo, Òbúko, Àkúko méta, odu-ara, leather bag, 16 bushes, àgbado, one ota, two leather Tọbílleras with 8 bells and 8 dilogunes each or with two bells and two dilogunes each. It is according to what is put on the anklets, because if diloguns are put on it, then two bells are

14

placed on the ẹbọ and vice versa. The Òbúko and Àkúko for Elégbà, the àgbo and Àkúko for Ṣàngó, an Àkúko for Òsányin (ozanyin). The bag is adorned with jujú of different showy eiye and inside it everything else is thrown and the Òṣa that ifá has determined is put.

To avoid delay

16 obí, 16 ewériyeye, 16 cocoons of ou, 16 silver pesos, a 4-color underpants or nightgown, rituals that are worn for 9 days and then presented to Òbàtála together with a 16-step ladder or steps, the obí are placed at the shore of the sea so that the waves take them away.

Artwork to Òṣosii

Òṣosii is lit with an ìtanná, anised or oti is blown on him and smoke is thrown from the asa and he is begged to free him and clear the way for him to succeed in life.

To thrive

Òbàtála is given adie méjì funfun, Òṣùn two Ẹiyelé funfun and then 6 ẹbọmisi will be given with: wild basil, rose piñon and prodigious and with that he washes down the house.

For Ikú to continue on his way

An Òbúko lerí, burn the hair and spread it on the face and in ṣilikun ilè, then with the lerí and the rest that Ifá marks,

15

make ẹbọ, open a kutun on the kitchen floor, place an aṣọ funfun where it is painted with osun nanaburuku Òṣé Tùrà, Bábà Éjìogbè, Òtùrà Ṣé, on this the leaves of Yaya mansa and encoma, iron files, are placed, the interested party with his lerí touches three times the lerí of the Òbúko used for this so that it replaces hers in front of Ikú.

Elégbà is placed next to the Kutun, obí omi tútù is given to the kutun calling Ikú, the Òbúko is sacrificed by throwing eyebale at Elégbà and what is inside the kutun, the lerí of the Òbúko for the kutun, the ará of the Òbúko is stuffed and sent to the foot of a ceiba tree. Opolopo epó is poured over the lerí of the Òbúko in the kutun, it is covered with a clay ikokó on which an Eegún atena is painted and ayanrìn is poured into the kutun until the ikokó is covered, then three okuta are placed, on top put on a burner and cook for 16 days so that the heat of the candle mixes everything inside the kutun and thus the lerí of the Òbúko that represents Àrùn and Ikú is recooked and leave the Awó Bábà Éjìogbè alone.

Secret for Ofikale trupon odara

Pine resin diluted in water, with the middle finger the Obírin is smeared on the clitoris, Bábà Éjìogbè is prayed.

Ointment for Oko for Ofikale Trupon

Camphorated ointment, iyé de iguí: Do not forget me,

16

larkspur and for me, pray Ogbè Tua, Ìròsùn Òfú, Òtùrà Niko, Okàna Òyèkú, Okàna Sa Bilari and Bábà Éjìogbè, spread on the glans before Ofikale Trupon.

Paraldo of Bábà Éjìogbè

This is made with Elégbà, it has all the ingredients of a Paraldo, a Ẹiyelé funfun, the usual ritual aṣọ, a gio-gio, in the aṣọ Òdí Fumbo is painted, a circle is made where Òtùrà Niko, Bábà Éjìogbè are painted, Okàna Òyèkú, the interested party stands next to the stroke of Bábà Éjìogbè with Elégbà behind and two lit ìtannás becomes Paraldo with the Ẹiyelé and the ewé: Carob, Purple Basil, Aberikonló (scares dead) and some more if he took them, finished the Paraldo everything is wrapped in aṣọ and then in cartridge paper, calling Elégbà and giving him a gio-gio that is thrown in nigbe with eku, eja, epo, àgbado, oyin, oti, etc.

Offering to Òbàtála through Bábà Éjìogbè

To make an offering to Òbàtála through Bábà Éjìogbè, the plate is prepared as for Ṣàngó, the sign Bábà Éjìogbè is written, obí omi tútù is given to see if he receives it and the offering is placed on the plate.

ALBA FOKEDE

This is born in Éjìogbè

Ifá says that a certain time that Òrúnmìlà was in the desert,

17

without water, without food, and his main interest was to find water, after a long walk he arrived at an oasis and when he got there the one who received him was Oddúa who, seeing him, threw the blessing in that way, then Òrúnmìlà began to drink water and when Òrúnmìlà was drinking the water he said, pouring water on his back: Alaba Fokete 0fo.

BÁBÀ ÉJÌOGBÈ PÀTAKI 1: WHEN OLÓFIN INVITED THE 16 MÉJÌS

Pàtaki

Olófin invited the 16 méjì to a dinner and Éjìogbè arrived late because he lived far away, and he needed to eat lerí de eja in the garbage, the méjì out of envy convinced Olófin to start dinner without Éjìogbè and despite committing They do not keep their share of it, when Olófin returns from the usual walk after lunch and sees Éjìogbè eating in the garbage, he makes him head 'If you eat head, you will be head'. This was where Éjìogbè became the first king.

BÁBÀ ÉJÌOGBÈ PÀTAKI 2: WHEN THERE WERE TWO MIGHTY PEOPLE

Pàtaki

There were two powerful peoples who were in continuous war with each other and Olofin, tired of this, sent different Òrìṣà to achieve peace between them, but they only achieved temporary peace, so he sent his favorite daughter Òṣùn with the task of achieving peace between the two peoples at any price, Òṣùn has to live with chiefs and soldiers of both armies to achieve peace, battered and disgusted by the okonrin, she retires to a secluded river (the avatar of Òṣùn Yemú is born there), where Yémojá goes to look for attention and care in his Ilè, already somewhat recovered and without adapting to the salty waters, he decides to return to his river, Òrúnmìlà, who finds out everything, goes to the river under the pretext of doing ẹbọ, pretends fall and allows himself to be saved by Òṣùn who comes to his request for help, Òrúnmìlà insists on giving him his ring (engraved with his Odù of ifá) and therefore claims her later as his legitimate wife (here the engagement ring is born), Òrúnmìlà acting with intelligence and tenderness makes Òṣùn happy, that is why Òṣùn is the Apetebí Ayafá.

19

BÁBÀ ÉJÌOGBÈ PÀTAKI: 3 THE FOUR UNMARRIED DAUGHTERS OF ODÙDÚWÀ

When Òrúnmìlà feels nostalgic.

Pàtaki

Òrúnmìlà was nostalgic to see his land again, which was the same as Olókun, Odùdúwà and Òrìṣà oko, because he had long since left it. That land was called IFE BO and when he arrived there, they were taking prisoner all the foreigners who were there, in whose raid Òrúnmìlà had also fallen, where he wondered: how was it possible that after so much time that he was missing from here I pass this on to me.

But Òrúnmìlà had seen this ifá before leaving and had made ẹbọ, with: Àkúko méjì ẹiyelé and other ingredients.

In that Òrúnmìlà asks a man what was the reason for that raid, and he replied that it was because of the governor of that place called Odùdúwà, who was angry, because his daughters had not been able to marry. Then Òrúnmìlà in an opportunity that he had, approached the governor and told him, you. He has taken us prisoner because others who have seen him have not told her the truth about why her daughters have not married. But I'll tell you: the first is blind, the second has a stomach ailment, the third has a lung disease, and the fourth likes women. Then Odùdúwà ordered to release all the foreigners and Òrúnmìlà in this way saved the town from him.

20

BÁBÀ ÉJÌOGBÈ PÀTAKI 4: WHEN ÒRÚNMÌLÀ LIVED IN THE LAND OF

Pàtaki

Òrúnmìlà lived in the land of Òṣà but away from it because Òṣà did not believe in Òrúnmìlà, but Èṣù whom Òrúnmìlà treated very well saw through a crack everything they did in the land of Òṣà and communicated it to Òrúnmìlà, certain time Òṣà challenged Òrúnmìlà to demonstrate his knowledge, but this one who had studied everything that Èṣù told him told Òṣà what they were doing without him being present, which is why Òṣà from that moment gave him moforibale. Seeing Èṣù everything that Òrúnmìlà had achieved, he asked him to do ifá for him, Òrúnmìlà told him that yes, bring him the ewé and Èṣù brought it all, missing two chivas, it's okay, I'm going to do ifá for you, but Èṣù clarified that two herbs that were Orozú and Coralillo were missing, Òrúnmìlà checked what Èṣù told him and then he told him: from this moment of each record that he makes, the five cents are for you, because you cannot be so greedy.

BÁBÀ ÉJÌOGBÈ PÀTAKI 5: WHEN ÒRÚNMÌLÀ WAS PERSECUTED

Pàtaki

Òrúnmìlà was persecuted by a tribe of unbelievers and was already lost, he took out his ifá that he wore in a sash around

21

his waist and placed it on the edge of a cave, which turned out to be the crab's, to prevent the unbelievers from taking his secret, kept running, but when he was cornered at the tip of a cliff, he jumped into the water, then an Octopus spread his ink and the unbelievers, seeing that, left him for dead. After the time Òrúnmìlà returned in search of his ifá and what would be his surprise when noticing the absence of his ifá in the place where he had left it, in this situation he began to moyugbar and the crab appeared that with its claws was giving him his ifá. It is because of this attitude that Òrúnmìlà told him: Neither you, nor your children, nor your offspring I will ever eat.

BÁBÀ ÉJÌOGBÈ PÀTAKI 6: WHEN THERE WAS A MAN WHO HAD MANY ANIMALS IN HIS HOUSE

Pàtaki

There was a man who had many animals in his house and many relatives lived with him, one day one got sick and died, everyone was sad except the kikiriki who had no reason to be sad, since death wanted to take her away, the owner of the house wasn't sad either because he knew the language of animals, one day the dog told the cat, don't run because I'm not going to do anything to you, because the master's wife is sick and we shouldn't be running around, the kikiriki He smiled saying: what cowards they all are at the moment that

22

the Lord needs them, none of them are of any use to him.

The day came when death came looking for the master's lady and all the animals were frightened, forming a tremendous uproar and screaming, but they fled to death, the kikiriki laughed at everyone and thus, laughing, he faced death and in one of his scrambles when he attacked her, one of his feathers got caught, death, who did not know what it was, got scared and started to run, but every time he turned his face he saw the feather and he ran more, in this way he chased away death and the sick was cured. The owner realized that the most intelligent animal he had in the house was the quiquiriquí, since he also knew the language of the saints.

BÁBÀ ÉJÌOGBÈ PÀTAKI 7: WHEN OLÓFIN WANTED TO CREATE THE EARTH

Pàtaki

When Olofin wanted to create the earth, he threw a kola nut seed and it fell into the sea, from it a palm tree emerged and the seven princes who took possession of the bud or flake, among them was OrannÌyán.

Şàngó, who was the smallest, and from the provisions that Olofin gave them, they distributed them, taking all the good ones and leaving Şàngó with a piece of land with cloth and twenty-one iron bars, thinking that they had kept the best,

Ṣàngó shook the earth Forming a mound in the sea, he released the hen that began to scratch the land and it grew on the sea and then it jumped to the land taking possession of it. The princes, seeing that what Ṣàngó had was more effective, since they could not govern without land, they tried to take it from him, but the twenty-one iron bars became defensive bars and he, taking a sword, advanced decisively on them, where the princes they argued that he had to share the land with them but

Ṣàngó replied: it's okay I'll share, but I'll be the one who governs. This is how Ṣàngó distributed the land forming the city of Oyó where he settled his first dynasty.

BÁBÀ ÉJÌOGBÈ PÀTAKI 8: THE WAR BETWEEN THE SON OF OBE AND THE SON OF ARA

Pàtaki

Obé's son and Ará's son had gone to fight several times, and Obé's son had always lost the fight, it was known that Ará whenever he fought, the earth gave him supernatural powers and for that reason Obé could not win him, for On the advice of his father Obé went to see Òrúnmìlà and saw this ifá advising him to make ẹbọ with: a spool of white thread and a black one, one hundred stones, three guabinas, eight slugs and a coidé jujú Òrúnmìlà told him that he was going

24

to have a I dream of a very pretty maiden and that later I was going to meet her, she would help him win the war of so many years that he had with Ará, but for that company he had to look for a ship, look for the head and listen to all the advice that they had given him, Òrúnmìlà told him that Ará lived in a labyrinth that whoever entered did not leave. Obé's son left very happy, he made the ẹbọ, he dreamed of the maiden, later he met her and she promised to help him, he asked for the borrowed boat to his father, he was going to the decisive combat and to carry a flag black, but that if he won he would return with a white one, he left with the maiden to his company and they arrived at the entrance of the cave, the maiden untied a thread from her skirt and told him to tie it around his waist so that she could guide him and could find the way out of the labyrinth, he entered and as ẹbọ had done, he found Ará asleep, taking advantage of it and suspending him in the air, strangling him, since Ará had no strength in the air. The maid began to pick up the thread and Obé's son was able to leave, but she was left completely naked, when Obé saw her, he felt completely ecstatic and they began to have sex, when they returned, he forgot to remove the black flag due to excessive joy What did you experience. When the father saw the black flag, he went crazy and threw himself into the sea, when the son landed crazy with happiness, the people told him what had happened to the father and remembered that Òrúnmìlà had told him to use his head and in honor of his Father, from

25

that day on everyone dresses in black. Birth of Mourning.

BÁBÀ ÉJÌOGBÈ PÀTAKI 9: BEGINNING AND END OF ALL THINGS

Pàtaki

There was a time when the saints, people and animals hated each other, they hurled each other among relatives, mothers and children, there was still no guiding belief and the saints hurled at each other.

There were religions such as Abakúa and Mayombe, but there was no head or prophet to govern and in the face of this situation Òlódúmarè was given an account, he seeing that the world was on the way to its destruction made a call to the people who he understood had destiny and they were responsible to govern, among them was Olofin, a saint of respect, for which Òlódúmarè gathered them all and asked them: what do they bring or have to govern. Among all the answers, Olófin only said: I bring heads and before this answer, Òlódúmarè gave him the command of the entire world for his government. Olófin tells Òlódúmarè that in order to govern he had to give him command of the stars, mainly the sun, the sea, the air and the earth, and a trustworthy person who was on earth. (These places are the 16 méjì, which are the 16 lands that he founded and toured and the compounds are the terms, of course each one has 16 different places), but in this tour of the last Olofin he realizes that he was being chased by a boy who transformed into different forms, before this Olofin calls him and asks him who he was, and he replies, I am Elégbà. Olofin replied, you are not Èṣù. and Èṣù tells him that what he was looking for was under the ground, and that it was in the first town that he had passed, realizing Olófin that this was the most hated place where people walked without heads tumbling, that is to say that they were phenomena. As in the last place where they were currently, it was precisely the place that announced that there were saints tied or imprisoned or disobedience to the saint. Olofin left with the boy who, in order to go, was telling him lies along the way, but he said a truth that he had seen, the place that Olofin was looking for and as he found it, he gave him the authority and gave him the name so that it would be together with him to resolve the affairs of the world and also told him that as long as the world was world, he would be the guide of all the questions of the people and is the beginning of all the future populations that will be founded. That is to say that Òrúnmìlà will be nobody without you, and you will be nobody without Òrúnmìlà.

Mferefun: Olófin, Èṣù, Eegún and Òrúnmìlà.

BÁBÀ ÉJÌOGBÈ PÀTAKI 10: WHEN INLÉ INDISPOSED HIS CHILDREN

Pàtaki

When Inle found Olofin, he upset his children in such a way that instead of giving them good advice he gave them a bad example, but although it is not possible for them to find children without a mother, he would show that without a father there could not be any either. Olofin withdrew the water from the sky for which reason the plants began to dry up, the earth cracking, the animals and people dying, then the children of Inle began to cry for the calamities that were happening and they presented themselves to Inle, and took an agreement who would promise to take a message to Olofin. The first to make the commitment was Aganjú the hawk, but when he passed from this planet to the other, the variations and the heat made him descend very dejected. He then promised to carry said message (Acha the Eagle), but the same thing happened to him, saying that he was willing to die on earth rather than climb up. Then Alakaso the Tiñosa decided, and she went up with the ẹbọ and overcame all the difficulties, although she lost all the feathers on her head on the trip, but at last she was able to reach heaven, and found the door open, she entered and found some water deposits and being thirsty he threw himself headlong to drink it. The father asked him what he was doing there and he answered that he was bringing a message from Inle and

28

his ọmọ for Olófin. He was surprised and said that they should bring her to his presence and told her that Inle was asking forgiveness for her and for her children that she was already convinced, then Olofin told Alakaso you have come and for that reason they are forgiven, go and behind Some drizzles will fall on you and enough water for everyone, this is the reason that Alakaso has the power to announce when it is going to rain. Before leaving Alakaso Olofin asked her why her head had no feathers and she told him that she had lost them on the journey due to difficulties, then Olofin blessed her telling her that she would find food before leaving her house, and that she would be respected by all. the governments of the world. That's why she finds her food before leaving her.

ẸBỌ: ẹiyelé méjì, akerebé, omí, jujú from alakaso, opolopo owó.

BÁBÀ ÉJÌOGBÈ PÀTAKI 11: THE BIRDS WANT TO IMITATE

Pàtaki

The Falcon and the Eagle are two birds that cause the envy of the other birds since they can fly very high, one day the other birds, driven by the envy they felt, met and agreed to make a bet with the Eagle and the Falcon, which consisted

29

of knowing who reached the peak of a mountain first, the section was short and since the Eagle weighs more than they thought, that it was easy to beat him, the day of the race arrived and everyone left, the small birds immediately achieved a great advantage away but very tired. After a while the Eagle and the Falcon arrived and ate all the smaller birds without their being able to avoid it due to their fatigue and the little resistance, they could do to defend themselves. Here the one who imitates fails.

BÁBÀ ÉJÌOGBÈ PÀTAKI 12: THE MBARRASSMENT OF ÉJÌOGBÈ

Pàtaki

It happened once that Òrúnmìlà was ill with his lungs and the hen attended him, took care of him carefully, but Òrúnmìlà stole his eggs every day and the time came when the hen began to notice the lack of her postures and she got into trouble. candle. One morning when Òrúnmìlà was accustomed to his daily robberies, it was for the eggs, and at the very moment in which he was committing such a misdeed he was surprised by the hen that told him: it seems unbelievable that you do that to me, I who have taken care of you with such care and selflessness, but you steal from me, hearing this, Òrúnmìlà left the hen's house embarrassed. Hence, Éjìogbè has to go through a great embarrassment.

30

BÁBÀ ÉJÌOGBÈ PÀTAKI 13: THIS PERSON WAS BORN FOR HEAD, ONLY ÒRÚNMÌLÀ SAVE HIM.

Pàtaki

This was where the head was alone and could not be saved, having a coconut business in the square, so Òrúnmìlà sent for coconuts and when he went, the head told him that he could not help himself and that he help her, Ṣàngó said yes, but he deceived her and did not solve anything, but one day Òrúnmìlà needed coconuts and went to the head, and the head raised his problem as he always did, and begged Òrúnmìlà not to deceive her, but he told her that he would not deceive her. She marked ẹbọ with food and as she was doing the ẹbọ, the arms, the hands, the box of the body, the feet emerged, thus emerging in this way the configuration of the body, and thus, in this way, the head could use.

BÁBÀ ÉJÌOGBÈ PÀTAKI 14: RIVERS ARE BORN HERE

Pàtaki

In this Odù Yémọjá and Òṣùn separated, Òṣùn spent many jobs and it was precisely when the rivers began to form, because wherever Òṣùn spent the night when he got up, a river was formed, that is why there are so many rivers and

31

only one sea. All rivers flow into the sea.

BÁBÀ ÉJÌOGBÈ PÀTAKI 15: THE BETRAYAL OF ÉJÌOGBÈ TO ORAGUN

Pàtaki

Olofin was blind and Oragun went to visit him, he always wears a leather jacket, but Olofin knew him because he passed his hand. Arriving at Olofin's house Oragun knocked on the door, Olofin asked who he was and Oragun replied: this, the son of his father, made him come in and asked him: what do you want son? I come for what he told me he is going to give me, come another day, Olofin replied, but Éjìogbè who was hearing and seeing him showed up the next day with a leather jacket just like Oragun's, he knocked on the door and Olofin asked what who he was and he answered as Oragun did. Olofin sent him to pass and asked him what he wanted, what you are going to give me, answered the false Oragun, I grant you the government and you will be the first for your good conduct and knowledge. Éjìogbè left and shortly after Oragun appeared, knocked on the door and Olofin made him come in and asked him, he answered what you were going to give me, Olofin angry told him: but if I just gave you the government of the world and You are not satisfied Oragun replied: father, but if you have not given me anything, where Olofin curses you and votes

32

you from the house. He leaves embarrassed and tearful, and on the way he meets San Lázaro and asks him what happened to him that he was crying and Oragun tells him everything that happened, and he tells him we are going to Olofin's house but Oragun refuses, but San Lázaro manages to convince him, when Olófin arrives he asks as usual who he was, Bábàlú Ayé your good friend, he sends him in and asks him what he wanted, no, I don't want anything for myself, I'm fine, I come to repair an injustice committed with your son Oragun and tells him everything that happened, to which Olofin replies: I can't do anything anymore because I already gave my word, but from today your Oragun will always be behind Éjìogbè.

BÁBÀ ÉJÌOGBÈ PÀTAKI 16: YEMAYÁ CREATES THE SWIRLS (Receive Olókun)

Pàtaki

This was where Yémọjá created the eddies in the water, since the hunters continually went and carried off large numbers of geese, and they did not leave them for procreation, but Yémọjá warned them not to take all of them, to leave some to be reproduced, but they paid no attention. To get to the island of the geese you had to cross the sea, but Yémọjá waited for them to return and when they came in their boats,

33

he created the whirlpools that swallowed the boats with the hunters inside.

BÁBÀ ÉJÌOGBÈ PÀTAKI 17: THE BODY GOT TIRED OF CARRYING ITS HEAD

Pàtaki

Once the body was married to carry the head and this with the feet, until the body said, do what you please, and each one prepared to do his will.

The head as more intelligent began to advise the body and how many vices and follies could make him see, that constituted joy, triumph until by that means he was weakening and had to sit in a place where the madman thought where else he could go, and then the The body began to do its own thing until the loss between the two was taking such a turn that Olofin said: I have made them both so that one is for the other, and they cannot continue like this, since then they have joined by order of Olofin. Despite this arrangement, we must realize that there are beings in the world that to please the body are lost and the same happens with the head. You have a disease in your body due to carelessness, you have to beg your head with eight different things.

BÁBÀ ÉJÌOGBÈ PÀTAKI 18: THE THREE POWERS OF THE SHADOW.

Pàtaki

La sombra estaba cansada de ser la menos considerada de la casa de Olófin vivía por debajo de todo el mundo, ni los animales ni los hombres la llamaban para nada, cuando ella se quejaba de esa diferencia le contestaban ¡Ay¡ si para verte a ti tengo que hacerte honores como a Òbàtála. Esta contesta hizo que la sombra llana de ira fuera a casa de Òbàtála a contárselo todo, pero éste le dijo que hiciera ẹbọ con un chivo, agua, tierra, Àkúko, tres cujes, genero blanco, ekú, eja, efún, meyo totu, tontu eyó ewé y que cogiera una palangana con ekó hiciera aṣé y lo soplara a los cuatro vientos la mar, el río, la tierra, para que todo el mundo la viera después del sol. La sombra hizo ẹbọ y es por eso que todo lo que está en la tierra la sombra lo ve, porque desde entonces la sombra adquirió los tres poderes que son:

1._ He managed to be a friend of death

2._ friend of the enemy

3._ savior of the innocent

It is for these three powers that the shadow discovers, covers up and kills.

BÁBÀ ÉJÌOGBÈ PÀTAKI 19: THE TWO BROTHERS

Pàtaki

They were two brothers, one older than the other, the latter being the one who governed the town, but, although the other brother did not show it, he envied his brother for the position he held, and made bad propaganda behind his back. One day, he gathered everyone in that place to tell him that his brother could not continue ruling because he was too old and that things were very bad, and he also told his own brother and he replied: you if you can do better than me, he handed over command to his brother and retired to the field to be quiet. The younger brother began his government, being such a disaster that the people agreed to look for the old chief, who made it a condition that, if they wanted him to be the chief again, they had to give him complete government.

BÁBÀ ÉJÌOGBÈ PÀTAKI 20: WHEN THE DAY WANTED TO TAKE THE LIGHT FROM THE NIGHT

Pàtaki

Before the day had more powers than today, the night was always his rival, the Owl as the most intelligent was the secretary of the day, to whom he entrusted all his secrets, but the Monkey was a faithful friend of the Owl, in those times the Monkey spoke and the Owl saw by day, one day, the day called the Owl to prepare a job, to take the light from the night, so that the night would have to pay taxes for having the sunlight, since the day he had the other stars on his side except the moon, which was the proudest of all. The day entrusted the Owl to write a letter inviting her to the party, the letters had to be written with acid so that the Moon when reading it would lose her sight and because of the glare the Owl had to put on a mask when writing the letter, the day and the Owl locked themselves up so that no one could find out about anything that was being plotted, when the Owl was going to deliver the letter to the Moon, he met his friend the monkey and said: look, by the way, I wanted to see you, that you it seems what the day wants to do, so proud, she told everything to the monkey, but the Tiñosa who was hearing everything flew away and told the Moon, which immediately came out in defense of the night, throwing all its cold light , but in that moment the sun came out in defense of the day and a tremendous fight began and everything was nothing more than discord, in that the day found out about the monkey and the Owl who had spoken everything and then the day understood that what had passed was very well used because nothing I know berry to do should be entrusted to no one, the day called the Owl and told him that as long as the world was world she would

37

not see the light of day again and that nothing that happened should be spoken, the Owl when reading the letter was blind, but the When monkey saw that, he screamed in fright that he was left speechless forever when he gave him the liquid he had prepared to drink that day, because they were talkative, one was left without daylight and the other without speaking any more.

BÁBÀ ÉJÌOGBÈ PÀTAKI 21: WHEN DISOBEDIENCE GOT TIRED

Pàtaki

Once the disobedience got tired, Òrúnmìlà and his father nature and by obedience to it, denied all the necessary movements to life, time passed and the food was running out, the animals died, the plants also dried up the rivers , it wasn't raining, the wind remained calm and didn't drive the movement of the stars, so the situation was dire, then Tiñosa, the most daring of all the birds and Olofin's errand boy, said: thinking like that we will die without any defense, and I decide what happens, it took flight and soared until it reached a desert, already tired of flying it went down to where a man named I have everything was, and he was missing a leg, an eye, an ear, and a hand. When Tiñosa found out the man's name, she made fun of him and told him: boy, you lack what we all have, and the man replied because that

38

wasn't his, he was just a cashier who kept the secret. La Tiñosa managed to get him to teach her the three secrets that were inside the three guiritos, which were air, water, sun, and wind, but in the last one there was a candle and she told him what it contained, which was what was scarce, and tasting a bit of soil, he told him to Àṣe to and the content came out. La Tiñosa praised him, and at the moment she forged a good friendship and she began to tell a series of lies to the man who fell sound asleep when she took advantage of La Tiñosa to steal her secrets. The tiñosa took flight and began to touch the wind, then the sun, and the water and when he went to touch the candle, it burned him, where the Tiñosa lost the feathers of her crown, running out of feathers on her head, When the The man woke up and noticed the robbery and went out to tell Olofin about it and he told him as a punishment: from now on and as long as the world is the world, you will be on earth and you will have the plants as friends, and they will be your food, and Tiñoza, for daring it will be hard for her not to have a fixed whereabouts and she will only feed on dead animals, and the water will drown her.

BÁBÀ ÉJÌOGBÈ PÀTAKI 22: THE EARTH WAS THE DAUGHTER OF A KING

I pray:

Ifá ni káfírèfún Èṣù, káfírèfún Òsányin, lodafún ilè Ògéré adífáfún Òrúnmìlà

ẸBỌ:

Osaidie méjì, adie méjì, a rat with a beaded necklace around its waist, shells, a doll with scarves around its waist, èbìtì, ekú, eja, Àgbado, obí, ìtanná, oyin, otín, efún, opolopo owó.

Distribution:

An osaidie with its ingredients for Èṣù, an osaidie with its ingredients for Òsányin, in the mountains if possible. Two adie with their ingredients for Òrúnmìlà

Note:

Eyebale is given to the ẹbọ, sending it to the mount along with the rest of the ẹbọ Articles, the rat with its beads and shells is released on the mount.

Pàtaki

On this path, the land was the daughter of a king, and she used to wear 200 handkerchiefs around her waist and said

40

that she would marry whoever saw her bare buttocks, where this news had to spread throughout the territory. The next morning Òrúnmìlà who lived in that place, became angry seeing this ifá and immediately remembered the phrases said by the earth, the daughter of the king. Òrúnmìlà performed ẹbọ and the aforementioned ceremonies, and by releasing the rat with all those beads, this caused an uproar, where people tried to see the rat fleeing towards the mountain. The land, hearing the comments of the people, went out to see the rat, where it undertook a tense chase because among the bushes and bushes, and with each step that the land took along the intricate path, it was losing its handkerchiefs, where it came to be completely naked.

Òrúnmìlà who was walking near her, when he saw her, he was stupefied at that vision of her, but reacting, he found her, when she sees Òrúnmìlà he said: What are you doing here? And this reminded her that she said that she would marry whoever saw her bare buttocks. The woman understood that it was true and she went to look for her belongings and she stayed living with Òrúnmìlà, and when she married the earth. She began to sing and dance happily saying: We have captured the earth and we will never abandon it.

BÁBÀ ÉJÌOGBÈ PÀTAKI 23: THE PATH OF THE PYGMIES

I Pray:

Adífáfún Òrúnmìlà, umbati unlo, ọba àṣe lówo Òlódùmarè orubo siwa fi àṣe ọkọnrin, kékéré ọkọnrin, umbati gbogbo aiye gergo pe otín akarà ṣe, lówo Òlódùmarè ni wó si ni wó oto gbogbo eyite owó ṣinṣe da ti gba a na wa ni oun ife àṣe lodafún Òbàtála bábà furuku òṣàlòfún.

Ẹbọ:

Àkúko funfun, ìleké funfun, obé of Bamboo, adofá malú, eye ni malú ekú, eja, orí, Àgbado, obí, oyin, ítanná, owó mérindilogun.

Pàtaki

In the land of Siguainle, lived an awó of Òrúnmìlà called Geokue Awo who was from Odù bábà Éjìogbè. This awó only received such bad thanks from him and nobody understood his thanks for the favors and works he did with them, so he decided to emigrate and go for a walk to the different surrounding lands, and in all of them what happened same. After much pilgrimage he arrived in a land where the men were of very small stature, they were Pygmies, Éjìogbè was welcomed very well and immediately they gave him work. He went to work in a slaughterhouse in

42

that town where he shared that job with his work as an awó, soon he had many godchildren among those men and it seemed that happiness smiled at him, but one day when Greokue Awó saw his sign, Bábà Éjìogbè and his fellow man's doubt resurfaced in his mind and he said to himself: I have to prove my godchildren and all those people who in one way or another owe me favors, so he took and smeared himself with blood from the slaughterhouse and went out to walk the streets. he knocked on his godchildren's houses and they opened and seeing him covered in blood they asked him what was wrong, and he pretended to say, I have killed the king's son, then everyone, full of fear, told him, please continue on your way, you are harming me , and Gereoke Awó ọmọ Éjìogbè had a heavy heart to see that all his affections were false so very sad he headed for the hills where there was a lonely little house painted white, where he had never been, he knocked on the door and an old man opened it dog bear who, seeing everything full of blood, asks him what is wrong, and Éjìogbè told him the same thing he had told the others, the old man invites him to come in to wash his clothes and feed him, and every day he told him Don't move son, I'm going to go to town to see how the situation is and bring you news. Until 16 days passed and Éjìogbè's conscience began to bother him that his fault was affecting the old man who was taking care of him, until he confessed the truth to the old man who answered him, I knew everything but I needed to give you proof that you

43

were alone and that you have me that I am Bábà Furuku Òṣàlòfún, the true owner of these lands and the one who is going to consecrate what you need in the lerí, he said, kneel down and he took 16 children out of his bag and crushed them with erú, obí, kolá, obí motiwao and he put it on the lerí and told him, put your ifá on the ground, but first write bábà Éjìogbè and took an Àkúko funfun, but first he took an Eja Bimbé smeared with opolopo orí, and put on the ifá of Éjìogbè and put the Àkúko in the lerí and prayed:

Bábà Éjìogbè boṣe adífáfún eja tútù yomilo

Bábà ororo Bábà ototo mokàneyi adele ni ifá

Olórun ototo kola yekun ototo moláyeifán

Bábà elerípin i ono balerí mola efún adele ni fá eri odara.

Then he took an obé of wild cane that he had in his hand, lined with fringes of Òbàtála and Ṣàngó and opa the Àkúko in the lerí that was falling in the Eja Bimbé and the ifá and he sang to it:

Eri eyeni Àkúko fokun Ifá nifá mokuaye

and he threw opolopo oyin and omiero from ewé from Aragba from Iroko, tenten ifá, dudu, Atiponlá, Ṣeverekuekue, guengueré oú, then he put Aṣo funfun in the lerí, and put it in the Eja Bimbé and sent it to onika and told him: today all day you have to be giving yourself ẹbọmisí

44

with that omiero, and he brought ayanrìn de sali. On the third day ọmọ Éjìogbè made osorde with his ifá and his sign was seen where Òbàtálá told him, take that ayanrìn, the Àkúko and the Aṣọ funfun that you had in the lerí and become ẹbọ ibin and take it to that Aragba and sing to her:

Erupintebo méjìro Éjìogbè ọbani Ikú aṣegun oluo indiri Olófin.

Thus, Éjìogbè regained his will to live and was able to recover the great power of stability and organization of the earth and since then he lived happily, although he knew that they were false to him.

BÁBÀ ÉJÌOGBÈ PÀTAKI 24: DIVINE JUSTICE.

Pataki

There was an individual who for a long time believed in the divine justice of God, but because he was looking at some things, which in his opinion were happening without apparently justified reasons, in accordance with the most perfect things of the omnipotent, he began to doubt the justice of god, and one fine day he picked up his things and asking came to Olofin himself: As god is the one who guides everything, he took care that the individual in question could get to where he was, and then asking him what he was

45

coming to , something that he knew too much, god proposed to said character to return to the world of truth, and to that effect, he provided food for some time and a new mount (an equipped mule), the individual in question went out to ride. After witnessing some things that according to his criteria had no reason to happen, he arrived at a grove apparently preserved to rest travelers, after choosing the place that seemed most suitable to him, he camped, unsaddled the mule and prepared to prepare his food, but while he was doing that he realized the arrival of another traveler to the same place and that after unsaddling his horse, he began to count a large amount of money, and while that was happening another man arrived behind him taking out a knife stabbed him ruthlessly, collected the money and galloped off. Witnessing this, which seemed quite cruel to him, he began to collect his luggage with the idea of returning to Olofin, to tell him that he definitely did not believe in him, nor in his justice while they had such events taking place, in that another individual appeared who upon verifying that the subject previously attacked had a knife stuck in his back, he tried to remove it and then the police arrived and arrested him, after talking for a while between them they pulled out a rope and hanged him, and this really filled the cup of the incredulous or doubtful man.

Saddling the mule he went to see God, who was already waiting for him with a series of documents and after listening to him he said: look son, divine justice always comes, and showed him how the one who was wounded in the house of the one who stabbed him killing him and collecting his money, because of the robbery the father of the one who wounded him had died and the one who tried to take the knife from him had been a partner in the assault, so it was agreed with the divine laws that the sentence of the killer had to be the death, and thus justice was served.

BÁBÀ ÉJÌOGBÈ PÀTAKI 25: OBATALA CONDEMNED THE ÀKÚKO TO DIE BY HANGING.

I Pray:

Adífáfún Àkúko Kay Kay Abele Bele Adie, Òbúko wa Àkúko Elele Kin Te Lese Oní Barabanirégún Agba Nilojé Ibeji nenu Awo Yeni Okete Foya Oluro Boşe Obele Adie Òbúko Wa Àkúko Lodafún Eegún.

Ẹbọ:

Àkúko Atitan batá, bgbo igi, gbogbo aşé, opolopo ìlẹké, ekú, eja, Àgbado, obí, oyin, itanná, opolopo owó.

I Pray:

Ibeji Ibeji Lórun Eti Ewé Ni Mosala Ibeji Eyire Miwa

47

Ṣàngó Mosaila Ibeji lórun.

Pàtaki:

In the Adie Miyeren land that Òbàtála ruled, it was strictly forbidden to kill Ekutele and they lived in a cave that was a sanctuary and whoever killed them paid with his life by decree of Òbàtála. In this land lived the Àkúko who was an important man and had great prestige among the men of that land and Òbàtála highly esteemed him. Àkúko was always at Òrúnmìlà's house, who in that land was called Awó Òrùn and when one day Òrúnmìlà made Àkúko bear for the first time, Bábà Éjìogbè saw him and said:

You have three things that you must take care of so as not to get lost, which are:

1. _ Ostentation and the cult of personality.

2. _ Women.

3. _ Money.

The Ibejis lived in that land and played near the Ekutele cave and accidentally killed some small mice, then they were horrified and ran away, they were crying because they knew that it was going to cost them their lives and that's when they

48

found the Àkúko Seeing them crying, he asked them what had happened to them and they, tearful, told him everything that had happened.

Àkúko told them not to worry, when they are discovered, I will tell them that it was I who killed them unintentionally and since I have so many influences in front of Òbàtála, nothing will happen to me and he will forgive me and thus you will be clean of guilt.

When Òbàtála found out what had happened and that the Àkúko said it was him, he said: The Àkúko is my friend, but he has broken my law, therefore he has to pay his guilt. Àkúko has to die.

They seized the Àkúko and sentenced him to die, that land was the gallows in a bush of Aragba that was on the outskirts of the town.

Àkúko had disobeyed the first thing that Awó Òrùn had warned him about. The day of the execution the whole town was gathered around Aragba, when they brought the Àkúko he looked at Òbàtála and for awó Òrùn and began to cry and with his tears a spring was formed that wet the feet of all those who were there, then Opa hanged the Àkúko.

Awó Òrùn, told all the Oşùn present that they knew of the innocence of the Àkúko, from now on everyone who is going to die for you, you have to wash their feet in

49

remembrance of the Àkúko, Awó Òrùn took some of that water and I pray:

"Abeye beye adie ni yero, ese wemo omí ye sokun àkúko.

Òsányin and Eegún were not present and were excepted from Awó Òrùn's predictions.

Since then, it was born that to kill àkúko, adie, ẹtu, ẹiyelé, akuaró, etc. Whether for Òṣà or for Òrúnmìlà, you have to wash their legs with prayers to erase the guilt and that everything is fresh.

Animals are not washed for Eegún and Òsányin.

BÁBÀ ÉJÌOGBÈ PÀTAKI 26: THE FIGHT ETWEEN EYO AND EKAN.

Pàtaki

One day the ẹiyelé lent owó to Ekan and since then she wanted to collect it every day, but Ekan did not return it because she did not have it. Eyo, in order to win ẹiyelé's friendship, offered to collect money and went directly to Ekan's Ilè and put his lerí inside the cave and began looking for Ekan, who, upon seeing him, began to defend himself with his pincers and thus was able to catch Eyó's lerí , that when feeling the pressure and not being able to get away, he began to force himself with his legs and tail, the ẹiyelé saw this and believed that it was the Eyó who was winning the fight, because of the whipping that he gave with his tail outside the cave. At last, Eyó managed to get the lerí out of the cave and the ẹiyelé observed how it was all bloody and with deep wounds, Eyó said: Because of you, look with Akan, he put the lerí on me, the ẹiyelé told him: boy when I saw the lashes you were giving outside the cave, I thought you were the one who was winning the fight. If you couldn't for you to get in.

Ifá says: that you do not get into other people's problems and do not charge or carry errands. You can't get into any house no matter how confident you are. You cannot enter dark houses. Food or pay the debt with Òbàtála. Don't let children drag things into your house.

BÁBÀ ÉJÌOGBÈ PÀTAKI 27: DO NOT KILL ANIMALS WITHOUT CONSULTING ÒRÚNMÌLÀ

Pàtaki

This road is where there was a town in the Takua land where three Awó lived, one was of clearer intelligence than the others and he worked for the governor, for which the other two Awó were fighting with him and arguing as a result of the envy. One day an individual sent by Eshu was presented to each of the awó so that the fight would end, when they made him osode this Odù Òsóìbò came out to each of the aleyos. After making ẹbọ, two of the awose killed the animals without consulting Òrúnmìlà. The other awó, who was called Ifá Ṣùre, did not kill them that day, but rather asked Òrúnmìlà and Òrúnmìlà oriented him on the day he should do it, so that neither he nor the person he was attending would have any difficulties, instead the awó who had sacrificed animals that same day, they did badly, one got sick for a long time and the other died.

This happened because death went every three or seven days to the house of the iworos and the Awo who lived there.

Note:

The awó should not kill animals for pleasure in this Odù and on this path, he wonders if he kills himself after seven days.

BÁBÀ ÉJÌOGBÈ PÀTAKI 28: OLÓFIN AND THE CHILDREN.

Pataki

Olofin one day took the children to heaven, because here on Earth they were mistreated and in punishment the Omi suspended the earth putting Eṣù as guardian. When the water on earth ran out, because it did not rain, the situation

52

became desperate, in a short time the inhabitants of the earth and the saints gathered together and decided to go to heaven to ask Olofin to forgive their children, but it was impossible to get to him. Yémojá transformed into a Gunugun here on earth and went directly to heaven to see Olófin. When Yémojá arrived in heaven she was extremely tired and thirsty and began to drink water in a pestilential puddle that Olofin found when he saw her, he took pity on her and remembered his children who were on earth and decided to forgive them and immediately sent the omi, but little by little so that there would be no misfortune. That is why when the saints come, they are given omí because they come thirsty.

BÁBÀ ÉJÌOGBÈ PÀTAKI: 29 PILGRIMAGES OF ÉJÌOGBÈ, WHERE ÒRÚNMÌLÀ GIVEN AROUND THE WORLD.

I Pray:

Bábà afofó bábà aroró adífáfún ọṣùn Lodafún Òrúnmìlà káfírèfún Olókun lodafún Olófin Ṣàngó Oluo popo, owó pipo, Èṣù, Olókun, Oluopopo alafia Òrúnmìlà unjen ogú.

Note:

The ọmọ of Éjìogbè are very addicted to oló from time to time and to oyu.

Pàtaki

This was an awó ọmọ from Éjìogbè who had many arayés who threw ogu at him wherever he went, he had to leave immediately for the ogu taught by the arayé who would not leave him alone, this awó always made osorde but never did ẹbọ complete and Èṣù always asked him for something and he didn't give it to him and the same thing happened with Alafia. This awó looked so bad that he had to go to Ilè loya a ole to be able to unyen, but aṣelú had been persecuting him for a long time because the arayé reported it. It happened one day that one night when Odubule awó an àgbo with Olófin, where he told him to give him obí méjì together with Elégbà and then osorde and whatever ifá told him to make it complete. When he finished odubule, obí méjì was given to his eledá as Éjìogbè was seen that marked him ẹbọ with ẹiyelé méta funfun, lerí de ekú méta, lerí de eja méta, ọfà, ifá marked him to take him to three different points of Ilè Olókun and when he came back from carrying the ẹbọ for yeyeé with ẹyin adie méta and threw it in Ilè loya, Ilè ibú, Ilè oké and when he made 7 Odù he had to unló from that land. When making the journey from that land to another, the awó found out that little by little I became otokú. In the new land the awó improved a bit of luck, after 16 days of being in that land he had an alá with Òrúnmìlà, where he told him everything that happened to him (work), etc., and that in everything that was he put in, ọfò came out, that aṣelú was

54

chasing him. When the Odù bule passed, the awó realized that everything was true, which was indicated to him since he still went to Ilè loya every now and then to olé, osorde and he saw Éjìogbè intorí aşelú lese arayé and that orugbo with jujú from alakaso marun, 25 ataré, 25 abberé, ekú, eja, 5 adie Òşànşara, lerí dudu and funfun, 5 ayé, akokàn de alakaso, ogui meyo, gbogbo tenujen, unyen owó meyilá otun, awó osi.

Then he told him that ẹbọ lodo ibú losa, besides that he had to oşişé Òsányin méjì okàn with 5 jujú from alakaso, to each jujú he had to put 5 aberé, 5 ataré and jujú from each adie for each alakaso and an aye in each jujú, ou dudu and funfun, iyefá that this Işé had to go to the foot of Elégbà and Ìyálóde or behind ilekun.

The other Òsányin is to carry it on, akokàn from gunugun, ou dudu and funfun, igi meyo iguiani, adie marun are for Ìyálóde in Ilè ibú and to call Ìyálóde in Ilè ibú with agogó, agogó goes in the ẹbọ along with the rest.

When the awó orugbo was not that ẹbọada and tired of asking, eleda put himself in osun and then Ifá told him that he had to osorde to the edun méta and unló for another land, he obeyed and went to another land and when osorde saw Éjìogbè, osalo forbeyó and Ogbètua, intorí Ọfò lese aleyo, the awó felt Àrùn de eleda and went to odubule without finishing osorde and wing with Elégbà, the wing was hard

55

and the frightened awó went to continue osorde if'a told him oño ẹbọ osaidie okàn lebo, 21 ataré, aberé méta, 3 pods of ejese, oto, a passán of ewé aroma, ìtanná okàn that before orugbo is turned on to Elégbà in addition to ewé almácigo, odan oyouro ewé la méta. When the awó finished, he took the opkele and put it on Elégbà and Osaidie was going to give it to him, but without removing it as ifá had told him, likewise, according to ifá's instructions, he put the abere méta through enu and the names of the araye, the 21 tie from behind and with the pass of ewé aroma execute them and put the three pods of ejese to Elégbà.

Note:

Eyebale who gives the osaidie when executing with him they pass, gives it to Elégbà and he took the osaidie and put it in the ẹbọ and then took it to nigbe and he did so. Where ifá told him that when he returned like him awó otun, awó osi, he would go ọmọ and then bathe with ewé, and thus the araye were running out before the year. The awó got scared and took a ẹyin adie, an osaidie, an ìtanná, he made a sarayeye with the ẹyin adie and Oke gave it to him and with the gio gio he also made a sarayeye, opened it and put it on Elégbà together with ìtanná and then there was oborí ẹiyelé méjì, obí méjì with ìtanná efún ewé ou, ewé tètè, emisi misi and agogó méjìla, from erú komalo after this he went to odubule and had a wing with Èṣù, Olókun, Ṣàngó and

56

Ounmila and Eegún from bábà Tobí where they told him that he had defeated his arayes, but that he had to give Òrúnmìlà euré and they join Òsà and Eegún. The awo the following edun gave moforibale to Òrúnmìlà and Òsà very early, he turned on ìtanná to Eegún and Eegún from bábà tibí begging them to help him fulfill all of them, after this operation osorde was made and Éjìogbè was seen, Ifá marked him the same as wing but adding that he had to give unyen to Èsù from itá méta, to gbogbo Eegún àgbo and angutan before leaving for the new land and that when he arrived he had to orugbo with Àkúko méjì, adie mefa, Eiyelé marun etu meri, kuekueyé, osaidie méta, saraekó, ekú eja, ilá, amalá, ere, oyin lese olerokuakue, aban aparó méjì, sila and amalá to Sàngó osaidie to Elégbà, osaidie for oparaldo. All the animals of orugbo are for Òsà and Òrúnmìlà osidie is for Èsù in ita méta and that all the animals will take them to their destination.

Ewo akuaró méjì, ilá amalá be given to alafi, take it to igi okue to speak with alafi there, take an adie kékére Tobíno and give it to inle afokàn yeri that when Olórun came out do nangareo take an Àkúko give it to him to Elégbà, Ògún Òsósii and osun, and to Òsányin he gave Àkúko, eiyelé mérin to oddúa, when the awó arrived at igi okue he put the order of alafi, okonrin méjì orubo presented him with moforibale and they told him everything that happened in those lands and how bad they were there that there were ikú,

57

arun, eyó, and ọfò, etc. They told him that they were going to take him to where the obá was from there, but since it was very late, he had a wing with Èṣù, Ṣàngó and sakuani and they at the ilá told him that they were going every once in a while, to make osorde and see Éjìogbè. Ifá told him that he would come to look for him but that before going he had to put saraekó on all the Òrìṣà and Òrúnmìlà and he did so and the Òrìṣà came to look for him and it was where the ọba ọfò eleda was but Ifá spoke with his ọmọ (ikú). The awó told the ọba that before Odù méjì he had to give ẹBọ to his ọmọ so that he would not otokú and told him that all things were ọfò that ikú, Àrùn, ọfò, eyo had gone, that the ẹbọ of his ọmọ was ẹiyelé okàn abuye owó meni tenti eni. The awó went to his osode and saw Éjìogbè that edun came to the awó's house to give him modukue for the unyen he had given him and to find out how he was.

Then the awó told the three Òṣà what had happened with the obá ọfò eleda, and they told him to leave it to his account that within 7 days the ọmọ of the ọba otoku, seeing this the ọba sent for the ọkọnrin orugbo for them to go look for the awó but he had become oborí and had a wing with alafi, Èṣù and Oluo popo, where they told him what they had done to him. The ọkọnrin orugbo begged the awó so much that he agreed where the ọkọnrin orugbo told them that they wanted him to advise the ọba that yoko Òṣà and untafá

58

Òrúnmìlà so that he would not otoku like his ọmọ. Being adumbule said awó, the ọkọnrin orugbo arrived, the awó was accompanied by them and when the bear of the ọba told him ona lese Òṣà and untefá Òrúnmìlà, he also told the ọba that first he arugbo with 16 ẹiyelé that are for Olófin, ekú efún, orí, Aṣọ funfun, who later had to go to the land of ifá, left for that place and the ọba yoko Òṣà and untefa at 7 eddun. When they finished untefa, the ọba received a message telling him that in his land things were going great but that Ṣàngó, Èṣù and Oluo popo had stayed there fixing everything, when the ọba found out he told the awó that he had to go with him there. When they arrived, the ọba named the awó head of that place after giving an extremely splendid party. The awó sent for Èṣù and told him to start ifá you have to give him unyen, but to you first, he sent for Ṣàngó and told him you also have to give you unyen méjì before starting any ifá to Oluo popo he said and you are the head of intorí Àrùn for any reason of that nature you have to count on you and each one of the orugbo was given a position to take care of ilèkan, thus giving rise to odan imole of Ogbèni. Note: This path belongs to Éjìogbè but it can be applied by another sign if Òrúnmìlà takes it, take a flat plate and another deep one, a piece of aṣọ pupa, the letter is ruined with Àkúko funfun and others, I know opa the Àkúko on the plate putting the name of the person inside they put epó and oyin on the two wings, legs and head.

59

Àkúko puts it in a jar with water and at night he votes for it on the street, calling the name of the person in the name of Şàngó and another saint, who picks it up the next morning, takes the plate with the goods to the mountain, they put it there calling the person asking for what they want, the deep plate is placed under the interested party's bed, putting the name of the person they want and a pink flower underneath and leaving it there for more than two days if necessary.

Note:

If Éjìogbè ikú comes out to an alòṣà or Bábàlawó, orugbo is made with agualebo, adie funfun, aṣọ funfun (3 varas), Aṣọ abowe métanla. When he finishes, orugbo will ask himself if agutan is for iyaré, and if he takes it, it is for when he finishes, he wraps himself in orí and abwa as if he were arupin and sends it to nigbe. FIN (dialect not understandable and poorly written).

BÁBÀ ÉJÌOGBÈ PÀTAKI 30: HERE ÒRÚNMÌLÀ FELL IN LOVE WITH THE ÀKÚKO'S WOMAN.

I PRAY:

Òrúnmìlà ṣoko fọbae inle adie eru ote koko boko ro la adie eru dada del olo ake yebi Òrúnmìlà yio adie eru Òrúnmìlà rofa abaní koto to ṣegun oda abani Ifá laṣe adífáfún Olófin

ẸBọ:

Àkúko, adie dudu méjì, ekú eja. Àgbado, oti, osi, ìtanná, malaguidi, ọkọnrin ati obìrin opolopo owó.

Pàtaki

It happened that Òrúnmìlà was in a bad situation and decided to go to another town to see if he could improve and find development until he reached a town until he met unkenaun kéké and asked him what his name was and he answered him little lion, my father's name is lion and my mother's name is lioness and Òrúnmìlà said, this land does not suit me and continued on his way in search of another place, when he reached another town he met an Ekùn kéké and asked him for his name and he told him, my name is my mother is called a leopard and my father is a leopard, and Òrúnmìlà said to himself that this town is not suitable for me either and he continued on his way arriving at another town where he found a little chick to whom he asked what his name was and he answered my mother's name adie dudu and my father Àkúko and my brothers the eldest asaidie and abebo adie and where do you live gio gio?, me on the hill, can you take me home?, yes, of course, follow me and Òrúnmìlà following giogio started walking until they arrived at the house where I waited Raba adie, Òrúnmìlà seeing that woman so beautiful and attractive Òrúnmìlà was impressed with her and said: lady if you would allow me to spend a moment to clean up and eat something because I haven't done it for days and she replied, good for that you have I had to see my husband kikiriki for him to authorize it, so I waited outside, this did not sit well with Òrúnmìlà, because he presumed that women did not resist him but he did not know that anyone was a woman of order and decided to wait. After a while of being there he saw a person who was coming down the road and he said to himself this must be the Àkúko because he walks just like the chick and he met him and told him what he had talked to someone else and the Àkúko told him: you can stay but when the rooster said this to adie aru he did not like it, he is wearing a great lady of his house he did not object but Òrúnmìlà was deeply impressed by adie eru and after bathing they sat at the table and Òrúnmìlà began to make jokes without that adie put the slightest interest and after drinking coffee adie and the Àkúko retired to rest since the Àkúko was a worker and had to get up very early. The rooster got up at dawn and Òrúnmìlà, who was greatly upset by the indifference of the lady, took advantage of the fact that the rooster had gone to work and entered the lady's room trying to kiss her, but she resisted and threatened to call the rooster. When the Àkúko came, they had breakfast and told him: good friend, I'm going to work and I can't leave you here, I'll show you where you can get a job and where you can sleep, so they did, but Òrúnmìlà was not satisfied since no woman had resisted him. and to avenge his wounded dignity a plan was drawn up he went to the semi-savage town and there he takes out his Òpèle it makes osorde coming out bábà Éjìogbè, when the people saw that they began to proclaim the fortune teller, Òrúnmìlà spoke to him and told him that he was going to take him out forward and began to do ẹbọ and the whole town acquired a lot of involvement but Òrúnmìlà did not stop thinking about adie eru one day he ordered everyone in the town to gather and told them: you have to go to the town next door and kill everything the world except for the woman who lives on the hill they bring her alive, Òrúnmìlà had consecrated an ifá to the chief of that town and his name was Ofun susu and he went to the front of the warriors and they finished and took the adie dudu and he takes it They went to Òrúnmìlà and when she was in front of him she began to offend him, and Òrúnmìlà told him: so much that you made me suffer and now I have you and the adie kept refusing Òrúnmìlà's caresses, spitting on him and slapping him, then he ordered Ofún susu to tie her up and He ate it. Olófin who knew what was happening said to Òrúnmìlà: because of the abuse you have committed while the world is world you will only eat adie dudu and Ofún susu will persecute you the curse of adie dudu and you will only be able to eat for the peace of your people adie funfun , Ofún susu became angry like crazy and it was necessary to urgently give someone a quick funfun on his head to appease the land of bábà Éjìogbè and Ofún susu, then Olófin said to Òrúnmìlà: to remind you of your commitment to the Obìrin,

63

put each one of them juju of I read adie in his lerí and you say to him: juju lerí adie Apètèbí abana and then he told Òrúnmìlà, so that ifá does not wear ọfò take epó and the league with adie's fat and pass your hand to your ifá with all this.

Note:

All women are desired, even those who have a commitment, women are raped. It is born that Òrúnmìlà only eats adie dudu by Olófin's sentence and passes his hand to ifá with epó bound with adie's fat so that he does not put ọfò, in remembrance of the abuse that the Àkúko woman committed with adie dudu.

BÁBÀ ÉJÌOGBÈ PÀTAKI 31: THE RED ROSE AND THE VEIN SACRIFICE OF ÉJÌOGBÈ.

Pataki

Once upon a time there was a man who fell madly in love with a princess and harassed her so much until he told her one day that he was madly in love with her, and she told him that he was not her height, that he was inferior because she was a princess and He also told her that he would only get her when he was rich enough to make her happy. Said man left for distant lands where, experiencing hardships and disappointments, little by little he became rich. One day after walking that land he entered the forest to try to increase his

64

fortune with its wealth and there he ended up becoming immensely rich. Working like this in this way, every time he remembered his beloved, he was overwhelmed by great sadness and began to sing a strange melody which was heard by a nightingale who lived in those places and who, entranced by that melody, struck up a friendship with said man.

The man told the nightingale his sorrows and the nightingale asked him to teach him the melody and thus they became great friends, but one fine day the man disappeared and the nightingale became very sad. When the man arrived in his land, he immediately appeared before his beloved telling her everything that had happened and that he was already very rich and that he was coming to marry her, so she told him that he should bring her a red rose to formalize the marriage, she knew very well that in all those lands there were no red roses, she told him so to delay the marriage. The poor man did not realize that this was a mockery on her part and that she did not love him. He goes out to look for the red rose thinking that he would get it easily, but no matter how much he walked he could not find it, so disconsolate and despondent he went to the forest and as soon as he arrived he began to whistle that strange melody, which was instantly heard by the nightingale that very happy he goes out to meet him and just seeing him understands the state of anguish in which his friend the nightingale is, tells him that since he had left he was very sad since he did not hear his melody and did not notice his presence, The man tells him about the anguish he was going through and what the real problem is that has led him to the forest. Then the nightingale takes a white rose and tells him: look, take this rose and if she loves you she will find this very beautiful rose, but he says no, it has to be a red rose, the nightingale says, look, go to rest, that I am going to pray so that tomorrow you find a red rose, when the man tired and dejected by fatigue fell asleep, the nightingale perches on top of a white flower and with its thorn the heart is pierced, staining with its blood the white rose, and remaining is completely red. The man wakes up in the morning and the first thing he sees is that beautiful red rose and he tears it off and runs to the palace, without realizing that at the foot of the rosebush is his friend the nightingale, lying dead on the ground, he only thought that he was He had performed a miracle at the request of his friend, and not realizing his friend's sacrifice, the man appeared at the feet of his beloved with that beautiful red rose and she then tells him, I never loved you, I only put this condition on you thinking that he would never reach her but the reality is that I do not love you and therefore I cannot marry you, when the man heard this he understood that all his sacrifices had been in vain.

The person who gets this ifá is told that all the sacrifice he can make for others will be in vain, he can even lose his life without realizing that others no matter how much he sacrifices himself, they will never take him into account.

BÁBÀ ÉJÌOGBÈ PATKIN 32: THE SUBJECTS OF OLÓFIN.

Pàtaki

The subjects of Olofin had the custom every morning to go to his feet to ask for his blessing, they kissed his hands, feet and the sacred tunic, thus demonstrating a true and mystical adoration of the father, to such an extent that he believed that this adoration of affection and affection was born from the depths of the heart, and that therefore they were sincere and self-sacrificing faithful.

Éjìogbè, who often frequented parties and meeting places and even the homes of many of them, came to understand that they were selfish, arrogant, envious, hypocritical and that each one tried to live as well as possible, even if they had to harm to others.

One morning when the subjects were paying the customary homage to Olófin Éjìogbè says: Dad, you do not know that this show of affection and affection is pure hypocrisy, to which Olofin replied, observe with what devotion they pay homage to me and this is irrefutable proof that they happily

67

abide by the moral precepts that I have dictated to them for their happiness and that of their descendants, if they were bad and hypocritical as you tell me, then they would not be able to offer me those proofs of gratitude. Éjìogbè was not satisfied and every morning he made similar insinuations to father Olófin and he, not believing him, pretended not to understand.

One morning Olofin, already tired of hearing such insinuations, waited for the subjects to give him moforibale and stopped them and in the presence of Éjiogbè he asked them: my subjects, I want to know if you love me and obey the commands that for your happiness and that of the others. I have taught you theirs. Then the subjects kneeling in front of Olofin responded. Dad, we love and respect you, we accept and obey your commands because we know that it is for our happiness. When the subjects left, Éjìogbè told Olófin, Dad, I do not agree with any of that, all this demonstration is pure hypocrisy, because if they are bad with each other, they cannot love you as they express, and with your permission, tomorrow I will prove to you once and for all that I am absolutely right. The next day when it was time for worship, Éjìogbè prepared a basket full of gold coins and stood to the right of Olofin, when the subjects were going to kneel to show their adoration for Olofin, Éjìogbè taking a step to the forehead and lifting the basket over his head, he threw it backwards, the subjects, seeing the amount of gold coins that were on the floor, rushed towards there and Éjìogbè had to quickly move Olofin away, so that with his haste the subjects they were not going to knock him down or give him a bad blow.

At that moment Olófin understood Éjìogbè's reasons and sentenced, Éjìogbè it is true that they are bad and that they do not love each other and have shown that they are false and hypocritical.

BÁBÀ ÉJÌOGBÈ PÀTAKI 33: OLÓFIN SUBIO A OKE A LAS 4 DE LA MAÑANA.

I Pray:

Emi tọbale bokun ogugu bele bui wí ako ola akoloko ko mi koko que adáfún, ibe tine ọmọ ayalórun aguere elebo Ẹiyelé ni orí, efu abere em jo Àkúko fifeṣù ebedilogun owó.

Note:

Òbàtála is the one who orugbo, this ọmọ is from Òbàtála legitimate and the first Messiah who loved the world.

Pàtaki:

Ifá says: that the three different people sent Òrúnmìlà to the world with the order to deceive the first children that Olofin had sent to the world. Òrúnmìlà complied with the order

69

and began to preach the doctrine to the first ọmọ of Olófin, these with different and true faith knelt before Òrúnmìlà every day and did all the honors they needed.

Òrúnmìlà in his preaching told them that one day he would see him arrive or come, but that, for this, they would first have to build an Ilè for him to see him and immediately afterwards he began to explain to them what the Ilè was.

Then Òrúnmìlà went up to Ayiguo and told Olófin that his children did not want to see or know, Olófin told Òrúnmìlà that the eternal Bábà could go down, but he had to caterpillar to be able to go down and this was with: Orí, efún, abere meyo, ekú, eja, Àkúko fifeşo. He made the orugbo and took him to 4 roads, at one point there was a blind man hidden inside nigbe and when Olofin was putting the ẹbọ, the blind man sank one foot and was for that reason calling a person, so that he would take away what that it hurt his foot and that he would give what they asked of him.

When the blind man came out, Olofin asked him what was wrong, and he replied that a thorn had been buried in his foot, Olofin pulled out the thorn and told the blind man: I need to know about my children and the blind man asked him, that where he was standing, Olofin replied that in the 4 paths or point (SM. Then the blind man told him to climb on top of Oke and look the other way, Olofin went up at 4 in the morning.

BÁBÀ ÉJÌOGBÈ PÀTAKI 34: ADAN AND EVA.

Pàtaki

Adam and Eve were companions and they were ordered to do ẹbọ so that, with the multiplication of humans at birth, so that with envy and ambition war would not arise. Eve made the ẹbọ for her, but Adam did not.

When humanity began to grow, envy and ambition arose and the fight with each other was born and when Adam returned to Òrúnmìlà's house, it was too late for him. And since then the man sheds his blood in war, while the woman gives it monthly.

BÁBÀ ÉJÌOGBÈ PÀTAKI 35: WHEN ÒRÚNMÌLÀ HAD NO WHERE TO LIVE.

Pàtaki

Òrúnmìlà had nowhere to live, they threw him out from everywhere. One day he went out with Òṣùn, to see where he could live, while both were standing on the seashore, Òṣùn watched as a whale wanted to eat some macaws, Òṣùn took his five Adams, threw them at the whale and killed it. The macaos in gratitude released their shells and gave them to Òrúnmìlà to live with oṣun. Note: the awó of this ifá carries two macao shells loaded with: Atitan Ilè erú, obí,

71

kolá, obí motiwao, gold, silver, ekú, eja, Àgbado, gbogbo
ewé, ayanrìn, they are carried after being loaded and live
inside ifá of the awo

He wonders what color beads are covered in this Isé.

BÁBÀ ÉJÌOGBÈ PÀTAKI:36 A RESPECT FOR THE ORANGE.

Pàtaki

On this path it is narrated that Atandá was the first Awó
slave with the Odù of Éjìogbè who came to Cuba and
because of his intelligence and ability he was the first slave
who gave him freedom. One of the richest landowners in
that region had to meet the slave Atandá, bought him and
took him to his residence, removing his shackles and having
him open and close the door of the mansion.

On a certain occasion there was a great reception attended
by the richest landowners in the region, Atandá being in
charge of serving them at the table and the astonishment
that this caused among the landowners due to Atandá's
composure was so great that it was the admiration of all, the
owner of the hacienda, in front of everyone he gave Atandá
the safe passage, where he signed the freedom of the slave
and all his belongings, he made Atandá see that if he read

that safe passage they would give him freedom, but since Atandá did not know the Spanish language he let said landowner know, and it occurred to him to make an Òpèle with 8 orange peels, which had also been served at the table, that he could read the present, the past and the future to all those present, which he did with They were all very wise and astonished, and they reached the conclusion and mutual agreement that due to their wisdom it was correct to give him the safe-conduct of his freedom, leaving Atandá in charge of the farm and all the servants. bre.

BÁBÀ ÉJÌOGBÈ PÀTAKI 37 WHEN OLÓFIN WANTED TO LEAVE THE EARTH

Pàtaki

Olófin wanted to leave the earth and sent for Òrúnmìlà, but Ikú also appeared and, unable to discriminate against any of his children, subjected them to a test consisting of spending three days without eating. The first day of them passed without difficulties, but on the second day in the afternoon the hunger could not be endured and Òrúnmìlà was sitting at the door of his house and Èṣù, who was the watchman, who was also hungry, appeared and asked him to Òrúnmìlà"; you are not hungry", Òrúnmìlà answered him; Yes, I am almost fainted, Èṣù told him: Well, let's eat; he told him: I can't do that, Èṣù told him: Don't worry, I'll take care of it.

Èṣù killed an Àkúko and two adie, cooked them and they both ate, collected everything and buried the leftovers. In that Ikú appeared to them, who came hungry and fainted and as he did not find anything to eat, he went to the garbage dumps, but Èṣù followed her and surprised her eating, so Ikú lost.

BÁBÀ ÉJÌOGBÈ PÀTAKI 38 IKÚ OPA TO THE HUNTER HIS CHILDREN

Pàtaki

A man, son of Òṣóṣii, went hunting on the mountain of Onikorogbè, but before he passed by the house of Òrúnmìlà, who saw this Ifá and told him: You have to do ẹbọ with all the eyin adie that you have in your ilè, so that you do not find yourself with Iku. The man did not make the ẹbọ and went into the forest and found no animals to hunt. After a long walk, he met Ikú and for a while they were hunting together. At last, they found two eñi alakaso (Tiñosa), and Ikú told the man: You can take them, but the hunter suggested dividing them, one for each one, but Ikú refused. When the hunter arrived at his house, he cooked the eñi alakaso and gave them to his children to eat, then Ikú arrived at the hunter's house and told him: I have come for my part because I am hungry and in Isalaiyé Òrùn we do not

74

have anything to eat, the hunter exclaimed: Oh me, we already ate the two eyin alakaso.

Then Ikú opa the hunter and his children.

BÁBÀ ÉJÌOGBÈ PÀTAKI 39: HERE THEY FIGHT THREE WAYS

Pàtaki

Here three paths fight: Land, Plaza and Water, because the three wanted to be the first, so the discussion between them was born; and the Ayá (the dog) who heard them, told them: you fight for pleasure, because none can ever be the first, because the three have the same right, so they must live together. When they heard him, they said: Well, explain to us better, the dog told them: All three have the same right because if the water does not fall on the land, it does not produce, and then there would be nothing to sell in the square. If there were no land, the water could not fall on the mass to produce. If there is no square, you cannot sell the fruits produced by the land from the water that fertilizes it. So, the three paths were satisfied and convinced. The earth told the dog: No matter how far you go, you will never get lost. The water told him: If the water falls you will not drown. And so, they were all friends of the dog.

75

Ejiogbe represents the sunrise in the East

2.- TRADITIONAL IFÁ ÉJÌ ÒGBÈ

BABA EJIOGBE VERSE 1

Ojúmó mo, mo rire; Kutukutu ijeni mo riwa-riwa; Diá fun Akapo; Won ni ko feja Aro bori; Ko too foju kan ire; Akapo feja Aro bori; Akapo foju kan're; O rire aje; O rire aya; O rire omo; O rire gbogbo; O rire aiku, baale oro; Nje aro, ara wa ro wa na o, aro o; Ojumo mo, mo rire rire; Aro, ara wa ro wa na o, aro o; Kutukutu ijeni mo riwa riwa; Aro, ara wa ro wa na o, aro o.

Translation

When it dawned I saw I will go in abundance; Very early,

four days ago my good destiny manifested; This was the revelation of Ifá for Akapo; Who advised him to serve his Orí with a live catfish; And he set his eyes on all the iré of life; The ire of wealth was lifted; And he will go from a good husband; And he will go from a good boy; And he will go from a good house; And he will go for long life, the king of all will go; Now Aro, we are very comfortable – Aro; The day dawned today I saw I will go in abundance; Aro we are very comfortable; I plow the catfish; Very early, four days ago, good manifest destiny; Aro, which are quite comfortable, the Aro catfish.

PROPHESY

Ifá says that, to be successful in life, there is a need to, among other things, serve your Orí with a large live catfish. Ifá says that if this is done, none of the good things in life will be missing. You will succeed where others have failed.

BABA EJIOGBE VERSE 2

Bu'kan mu; B'eji K'agba ki o mu'kan ko 'ra a re o; Ko le baa se jomu-regi; Bo ba wu mi; Na fi Ifa a mi fo Gemberi; Bo ba wu mi; Ma fi Ifa a mi fo Gambari; Ma fi fo Huku-huku; Ma fi fo Wenu-wenu; Gemberi ni o r'eru Hausa; Agbigbo ni o fon faa-faa r'ode orun; Dia fun Akalamagbo; Ti yoo te Olokun-Seniade n'Ifa; Ebo ni won n I ko se; O gb'ebo, o ru'bo; Nje t'emi oba logboogba; Oba ma n d'ade; Mo gbe'de bo'run; T'emi Oba logboogba.

Translation

Drink one (cup); Serve two for seniors; Serve two for the old man and one is served for you; For it to be fair and necessary; If I like it; I am going to use my Ifá to speak in the Gamberi language; And if I like it; I am going to use my Ifá to speak in Gambari language; I use it to speak in Hukuhuku; And speak-Wenu wenu; A Gemberi man does not bear the burden for a Hausa man; And an Agbigbo, don't shout out loud to the sky; Ifá Messages from Akalamagbo; When Ifá is going to be performed for Olókun Seniade; He was advised to offer ebo; He complied; The Oba and I are the same, The Oba wears a crown; I adorn the neck with Ifa beads; The Oba and I are the same.

PROPHESY

Ifá says that when he comes from heaven, that he chose to be a great leader. You chose to be numbered among the kings of the world. As a consequence of this, he was approved to be equal to kings, emperors, rulers and national administrators.

Ifá advises that the IDE, Ifá accounts, should be used at all times. You need to use the beaded necklace as it sets you apart from everyone else.

79

Ifá also advises you to offer ebo with two Irukere, cow tails, two white doves, two guinea fowl and money. It is also necessary to feed Ifá with a smoked catfish (catfish).

BABA EJIOGBE VERSE 3

Otootootoo; Oroorooroo; Otooto laa kole; Otooto laa gbè 'nu u re; Ogbon ta a fíí ko'le; Ko to eyi taaa fi igbe 'nu u re; Diá fun Orunmila; Níjo ti Ajogun merin ka won mole l'Otu Ife; Ti Baba le won, le won; Ti won o lo; Ebo ni won ni ko waa se; O gbè'bo, o ru'bo; E wa ba ni ni wòwó iré gbogbo.

Translation

Otootootoo; Oroorooroo; Separately we can build our houses; Separately is what we live in the houses; The wisdom with which we have built our houses; It is not as much as that with which we live in homes; These were the statements of a case of Orunmila; When four Ajogun; they invaded the city of ile-Ife; And they tried to throw them out without success; They just refused to go; He was advised to offer ebo; complied; In a short time, not far away; Join us in the midst of abundant successes.

PROPHESY

Ifá says that he foresees all the IRE all for you. Ifá says that death will be replaced with wealth, sadness with joy, sorrow with celebration, loss with longevity and desire with achievement. Ifá says that you should live and die as a happy man.

In this Odù, Ifá says that death turns into economic well-being, wife affliction, litigation to opportunities to have children, and loss of longevity. Ifá says that there is a need for you to offer Ebo known as ARUKORE or ARUKAPONJA. Materials include the sacrifice, 2 pigeons, 2 roosters, 2 rats, 2 fish, 4 Obi Kola, 4 bitter kola, 4 guinea peppers, and money.

BABA EJIOGBE VERSE 4

Apala nii so bi omu bi omu; Popondo níí so bi adaasa bi adaasa; Agogo ide níí bale; Níí ro jijiwowo-jijiwowo; Dia fun Obi; Ti nsawo rode Ekiti-Efon; Ebo ni won ni ko se; O gb'ebo, o ru'bo; Ewi-Ado jingbinmi l'omo Obi; Awimo-logbon jingbinni l'omo Owu; Iran awa o rin l'agan ri o.

Translation

Apala seed resembles a woman's breast; Popondo seed looks adaasa; A bronze gong fell and there was a clang; Ifá message for the Obi, cola nut; When he leaves on an Ifá mission for the Ekiti-Efon people; He was advised to offer ebo; He complied; EWI-Ado, abundant seeds is Obi; He who

81

teaches the wisdom of him devoted to him, abundant are the products of the anvil; Our generations never know that it is sterile.

PROPHESY

Ifá foresees that of good children for you. Ifá also predicts that you will be blessed with all the good things in life. you will not lack anything in life. Ifá advises you to be happy with what Òlódúmarè has blessed you. There is a need for you to offer ebo and feed Ifa.

Ifá advises you to offer ebo with a basket full of Obi and money. It is also necessary to feed Ifá with 16 Obi.

BABA EJIOGBE VERSE 5

Mimo oju Olorun ko kan gbigba; Ewa Osupa ko kan tiwe; Isanra Ose ko kan ti onje; Ofa fun Orunmila; Ifa nlo ree gbe Orilewa niyawo; Ebo ni won ni ko waa se; O gbe' bo, o rubo; Nje e sare wa, e waa wo omo Orilewa werewere; Orunmila lo gbe Ori lewa niyawo; E sare wa, e waa wo omo Ori lewa werewere.

Translation

The clearing of the sky is not the result of constant sweeping; The beauty of the moon is not as a result of a regular bath;

The bulk of the Ose tree is not as a result of frequent ingestion; These were the declarations to Òrúnmìlà; When she is going to have Ori lewa's hand in marriage; She was advised to offer ebo; He complied; Come see the beautiful children of Ori lewa; Òrúnmìlà is the same one who had taken Ori lewa as his wife; Here are the beautiful children of Ori lewa.

PROPHESY

Ifá says that he foresees I will go from a good wife to you. Ifá says that the relationship will be blessed with the progress of happiness, children and security. For this to happen, there is a need for you to offer ebo of 1 hen, 1 pigeon, 4 fish, 4 rats and money. Also, to feed Ifá with 4 rats, 4 fish, palm oil and money.

BABA EJIOGBE VERSE 6

Ominimini; Dia fun Omi-tutu; Ti nt'ikole orún bò wa'le aye; Ebo ni won ni ko se; O gb'ebo, o ru'bo; Nje kinla b'Omi-tutu ti nse?; Ominimini; A b'Omi-tutu ti nt'aye se; Ominimini.

Translation

Ominimini; Ifa was guessed for Omi-tutu, fresh water; When he came from heaven to earth; He was advised to

offer ebo; She did so; What do we find Omi-tutu doing?;
Ominimini; We find Omi-tutu fixing the world; Ominimini.

PROPHESY

Ifá promises that all the things that are giving you pain and
sorrow. Joy and satisfaction will be your lot. You will have
reason to rejoice.

Ifá advises you to offer ebo with 2 chickens, 2 pigeon
pigeons, 2 guinea fowl, 2 roosters and money.

BABA EJIOGBE VERSE 7

Ifá lo deni; Mo lo deni; Elénìní; Dia fun Lameni; Omo
atorun la gbegba aje waye; Ifa lo deji; Mo lo deji; Ejeeji; Dia
fun Sie-Ejide; To feyinti moju ekun sunrahun omo; Ifa lo
d'eta; Mo lo d'era; Ikorita meta abidi yakata-yakata; Dia fun
Tamilore; Tii somokunrin Ita; Ifa lo d'erin; Mo lo d'erin;
Erin ni won nrin fona Ori; Erinsese lagbara nrin ko'do lona;
Dia fun Eleinmagba; Omo atako leleele según; Ifa lo d'arun;
Mo lo d'arun; Oroorun ni won nkala; Oroorun ni won
nkakan; Dia fun Olorunjinmi; Oroorun ni won nfi ohun ire
e jinraa won; Ifa lo d'efa; Mo lo d'efa; Iru gbogbo lo nfiru
j'eta; Bi won ba denu igbo; Dia fun Olofa-Eta omo atako
leleele según; Ifa lo d'eje; Mo lo d'eje; B'Olugbon ba soro; A
kije; A'Aresa ba soro; A kije dia fun Olojele asote; Ti nbe

84

laarin ota; Ti nfojoojumo kominu ogun; Ifa lo d'ejo; Mo lo d'ejo; Kiwaju ile o jo sirere sirere; Keyinkunle ile o jo sirere sirere;

Dia fun Abinjo; Ti won bi sode igbajo; Toun ti Iresi oro; Iwa jo; Eyin jo; Mo ti sawo; Egbejo temi; Ifa lo d'esan; Mo lo d'esan; Asan-gbo laso tawon; Awo-gbo laso tawa o; Dia fun Alakesan-magba; Erigi mabga; Eyi to joba tan; To nsunkun oun o ri Olusin; Awa m'Alakesan je Oloja; Gbogbo omo eni; E yaw a, e wa sin; Gbogbo omo eni; Ifa lo d'ewa; Mo le d'ewa; Wiwa-wiwa n won nwa babalawo o rele; Babalawo kii wa enikan soso; Dia fun owa-oga; Owa ogirii gbedu; Omo okun yeye; A ja fibi kookoo lale; Eyi to nsunkun wipe apa oun o kaye; If lo d'okanla; Mo do d'okanla; Okanla ni won nderu f'Olu; Okanla ni won nderu f'Awo; Okanla ni won nderu welewele jako; Dia fun Okanlawon; Won ni ko rubo; Ki ekeji ree torun o le da oun rere lee lowo; Mo lo d'iji; Orunmila ni toun ba ji lorooru kutukutu; Ohun gbogbo lo maa nba oun laraa de; O ni toun ba ji loororu kutukutu; Toun ba maso dudu bora nko?; O ni won a ni Orunmila pele; Omo aladuu-ja; Omo oniwonran; Ifa lo tun d'iji; Mo lo tun d'iji; Orunmila ni toun ba ji lorooru kutukutu; Ohun gbogbo lo maa nba oun lara a de; Ohun gbogbo lomaa nba oun lara a de; O ni toun ba ji lorooru kutukutu; Toun ba faso pupa bora nko?; O ni won a ni Orunmila pele; Omo onile kan, ile kan; Ti nba won pon risarisa; Ifa lo tun d'iji; Mo lo tun d'iji; Orunmila ni toun ba ji lorooru kutukutu; Ohun gbogbo lo maa nba oun lara a de; O ni toun ba ji lorooru kutukutu; Toun ba f'aso funfun bora nko?; O ni won a ni Orunmila pele; Omo igi ope ka nope kan; Ti nba won fun ningin-ningin; Fia lo tun d'iji; Mo lo tun d'iji; Orunmila ni toun ba ji lorooru kutukutu; Ohun gbogbo lo ma nba oun lara a de: O ni toun ba ji lorooru kutukutu; Ohun gbogbo lo maa nba oun lara a de; O ni toun ba ji lorooru kutukutu; Toun o bob ante nko; O ni won a ni Orunmila pele; Orunmila nle; Pelepele omo arinhoho sosin; Pele omo arinhoho sora; Idi ni gbedogbedo ti m'odo o tire e gbe o; Idi ni ajao ti mu'gi ree gun; Ko too re ogengen igi; Idi ni Ara a mi Agbonijosu ti b'obinrin re sere; To ba digba ajodun; Ire omo nii yori i si; Dia fun Egbe; Dia fun Eran; Dia fun Sasara; Dia fun Aroni abosu panpa; Dia fun Sonakoki;

Ti somo Ikeyin won lenje-lenje; Won ni ki won rubo si laiku araa won; Won gbebo, won rubo; Nje bo sogun odun lonii; A ma ba won se bi lori Ikin je; Bo se ogbon odun lonii; A maa ba won se'bi lori Ikin je; Aadota odun lonii; A maa ba won se'bi loro Ikin je; Awa ti di Sonakoki; Iku kii pa asebi lori Ikin je; A ti di Sonakoki.

Translation

Ifá says that "now it is one"; I chant that "now it is one"; Eleeni; He was the Awo who launched Ifá for 'Láméní; The one who carries the gourd of wealth and success from heaven to earth; Ifá says that "now it is two"; I chant that "now it's two"; Ejeeji; He was the Awo who launched Ifá for Sie-Ejide; That he was leaning back and crying over his inability to have a child; Ifá says that "now it is three"; I chant that "now it's three"; The three crossroads with a broad base; He was the Awo who launched Ifá for Tamilore; Ita's son, from the main street; Ifá says that "now it is four"; I chant that "now it is four"; It is with the smile people pick up the fire for the distillation of liquor; With a smile, the flood joins the river; They were the Awo who launched Ifá for Elerin-magba, the king of Erin-ile; The one who leaves knots, bushes and grasses to overcome adversary; Ifá says that "it is five"; I chant that "it's five"; Every five days is what okro harvests; Every five days is what the harvest of garden eggs; They were the Awo who launched Ifá for Òlorun-jinmi; Every five days they present gifts to each other; Ifá says that "it is six"; I chant that "it's six"; All animals resemble Eta's tail; When they are in the bush; They were the Awo who launched Ifá for Olofa-Eta; The one who leaves knots, bushes and grasses to overcome adversary; Ifá says that "it is seven"; I chant that "it is seven"; When Olugbon performs his annual ritual; To be held on the seventh day of the ceremony; Every time Aresa performs his annual ritual; To be held on the seventh day of the ceremony; They were the Awo who launched Ifá for Olojele, the conspirator; When he was in the midst of enemies; And he lived in constant fear of enemies; Ifá says that "it is eight"; I chant that "it's eight"; That the facade of his house is calm and peaceful; That the back of the house is calm and peaceful; They were the ones who issued Ifá for Abimjo; That he was born in the city Igbajo; He and Irési gold; The front is calm and peaceful; The back is calm and peaceful; I have offered my own ebo with 1,600 snails; Ifá says that "it is nine"; I chant that "it is nine"; Their clothes are to be hung until they are in pieces"; Our dresses are to be worn until they fade; They were the Awo who launched Ifá for Alakesan-magba; The praise of the name includes " Erigi-magba; Who, after being installed in Oba; He was crying, lamenting his inability to have people pay homage to him; Now we have made Alakesan the head of the market; All our children; Step here and pay homage; All our children; Ifá says that "it is ten"; I chant that "it's ten"; The clients are those who go to the Bábálawo's house; Bábálawo does not often go to a client's house; This was Ifá's declaration to Owa Ogirii-gbedu; Descendants of those who greet with "Okun-Yeyé"; The one who fights and uses the handle of his sword to mark the ground; When he was crying, lamenting his inability to control his subjects; Ifá says that "now it is eleven; I chant that "now it is eleven; When packing materials for the Olu ritual, there are always eleven; When the packing material for the Awo ritual is always eleven; These were the declarations of Ifá Okanlawon; Who advised you to offer ebo; So his second of his in heaven fill him with gifts; Ifá says that "it is twelve"; I chant that "it's twelve"; Orunmila says that every time she wakes up at dawn; All things agree with it; He asks her what if she wakes up at dawn; And she wraps herself in a black blanket?; They respond that people say "gentle Orunmila"; "The man who glows in the dark about him;" The owner of black jewelry stores; Ifá says that "it is twelve again"; I chant that "it's twelve again"; Orunmila says that every time he wakes up at dawn; All things agree with it; He asks her what if he wakes up at dawn; And he wraps himself in a red blanket

They respond that people say "gentle Orunmila"; "Owner of the space of the earth"; "That's as red as mud"; Ifá says that "it is twelve again"; I chant that "it's twelve again"; Orunmila says that every time he wakes up at dawn; All things agree with it; Ifá says that what if you wake up at dawn; And is wrapped in a white blanket?; They respond that people say "careful Orunmila"; "The owner of that palm tree"; "Which is white and spotless"; Ifá says that "it is twelve"; I chant that "it's twelve"; Orunmila says that everything that wakes up at dawn; All things agree with it; Orunmila asks that everything wake up at dawn; All things agree with it; Orunmila asks him what if he wakes up at dawn; And he chooses to wear neither pants nor apron?; They reply that people greet him and say "watch out Orunmila"; "Easy of Orunmila";

PROPHESY

Ifá says that the wealth and prosperity and the person for you are foreseen. Ifá says that they have brought him his wealth from heaven. Ifá says that you are going to give birth

89

to a pair of twins or that you were born with a double that has twins in your lineage or that you are a twin. In a word, they are closely associated with the deity Twins. In the same stanza, Ifá says that you will have good luck throughout your life and you will overcome your problems and enemies, no matter how many they are.

Ifá says that you will also have tranquility and happiness in your life and that you will be in full control of your life and the lives of those around you. In the same stanza, Ifá says that you are an ELEGBE and that your celestial double will shower you with all the good things in life that will bring you success and achievement. Ifá also says that you will find comfort in any condition, no matter how harsh the situation may be. You will also win the admiration of others with the way you carry yourself in tough and difficult situations. Ifá also says that five children and five young people, whether biological or adopted, children will have a great influence on your life. Ifá advises however that it is necessary to offer sacrifices for the children in order to avoid dying young.

BABA EJIOGBE VERSE 8

Abede Awo Okira; Dia fun Okira; Ti yoo maa sowo aseti; Ebo ni won ni ko se; O gb'ebo, o ru'bo; Abede ma ma de o, Awo Okira; Ifa ma jee ki Okira o sowo aseti mo o; Abede o, Awo Okira.

Translation

Abede, the Awo of Okira; He made Ifá divination for Okira; When he was suffering from the problem of unconsummated fortune; He was advised to offer ebo; He complied; Here comes Abede, the Awo of Okira; Please don't let Ifa Okira suffer from the problem of unconsummated fortunes; Abede, the Awo of Okira.

PROPHESY

Ifa says that all unconsummated areas of fortune will depart from your life. You will be able to realize all your plans, goals and aspirations in life. You will always be successful in all your important undertakings.

Ifa advises him to acquire a gray rat, Èdá, and wraps it in a fresh palm leaf. He will place the rat on the main road and use a sharp knife to cut it in two with one blow. He must make sure that the rat is cut at once. If this is done, then unconsummated fortune problems will be removed from your life.

BABA EJIOGBE VERSE 9

Otootooto; Oroorooro; Otooto laa j'epa; Otooto laa j'imumu; Loto-loto laa so olu esunsun s'enu; Oun t'Ori ni t'Ori; Oun t'oori ni t'oori; Oun t'Ori-t'oori laa fi fun

Obamakin lode Iranje; Ko le baa foun t'Ori-t'oori ta'ne l'oore; Dia fun Egbaji arun; Ti ntikole Orun bo wale Aye; Eji-Ogbe ni o ji asiwaju won; Ebo ni won ni ko waa se; O gb'ebo, o ru'bo; Ko pe, ko jinna; E ba ni laiku kangiri.

Translation

Otootooto; Oroorooro; Separately, peanuts are eaten; Separately, tamarinds are eaten; And separately, it eats the queen bees; What belongs to Orí is Orí's; And what is Oori's is for Oori; But what is common to both Orí and Oori is what we give Obamakin Iranje on earth; To bless us with what is for both Orí and Oori; Ifá message for the 4000 diseases; When it comes from heaven to earth; Èjì-Ogbè was their leader from heaven; He was advised to offer ebo; They complied; In a short time, not far away; Join us in the midst of eternal victory.

PROPHESY

In this verse Ifá says that there is a need to ensure special preparation for you, in order to avoid experiencing incessant ailments. Ifá says that his Odù, Èyì-Ogbè, is the leader of all evil from heaven to earth. That is the reason why you may experience incessant disturbances. There is a need to prepare a special Ifa medicine, in the interest of putting an end to these evils. Ifá advises to offer ebo with: an adult goat, 2 Guinea hens and money. After this, you have to look for Ishú, Elú, indigo, 16 land snails and Pèrègún leaves. And feed Ifá with the 16 snails, and the league of Elú, Ishú and Pèrègún together, mix with soap and water. Then you will use the juice of the land snail, to mix with the soap very well.

BABA EJIOGBE VERSE 10

Mo sa pamo, sa pamo; Orí mi loun o sa pamo; Mo rin ni koro, ni koro; Èdá mi loun o fe koro; Dia fun Ilé; Nijo ti o torun bo waye; Won ni ko rubo; Ki nnkankan ma baa gorii re; Ile ni aye ti ye awon to bayii; Ojo naa ni won te Eni lee lori; Mo sa pamo, sa pamo; Orí mi loun o sa pamo; Mo rin ni koro, ni koro; Èdá mi loun o fe koro; Dia fun eni; Nijo ti o ntorun bo waye; Won ni ko rubo; Ki nnkankan ma baa gorii re; Eni ni aye ti ye awon to bayii; Lojo naa ni won te ite lee lori; Mo sa pamo, sa pamo; Ori mi loun o sa pamo; Mo rin ni koro, ni koro; Eda mi loun o fe koro; Dia fun Ite; Nijo ti o ntorun bo waye; Won ni ko rubo; Ki nnkankan ma baa gorii re; Ite ni aye ti ye awon to bayii; Lojo naa ni won gbe Apere lee lori`; Mo sa pamo, sa pamo; Orí mi loun o sa pamo; Mo rin ni koro, ni koro; Eda mi loun o fe koro; Dia fun Apere; Nijo ti o ntorun bo waye; Won ni ko rubo; Ki nnkankan ma baa gorii re; Apere ni aye ti ye awon to bayii; Ojo naa ni won gbe Apere lee lori; Mo sa pamo, sa pamo; Orí mi loun o sa pamo; Mo rin ni koro, ni koro; Èdá mi loun o fe koro; Dia fun Oba; Nijo ti o ntorun bo waye; Won ni ko rubo; Ki nnkankan ma baa gorii re; Oba ni aye ti ye awon

93

to bayii; Ojo naa ni won gbe Ade lee lori; Mo sa pamo, sa pamo; Orí mi loun o sa pamo; Mo rin ni koro, ni koro; Èdá mi loun o fe koro; Dia fun Adé; Nijo ti o ntorun bo waye; Won ni ko rubo; Ki nnkankan ma baa gorii re; Ade ni aye ti ye oun to bayii; Ojo naa ni won fi Iye Okin; Mérìndínlogún (16) gun lori; Mo sa pamo, sa pamo; Orí mi loun o sa pamo; Mo rin ni koro, ni koro; Èdá mi loun o fe koro; Dia fun Iye Okin merìndínlógún; Won n ntorun bo wale aye; Won ni, ki won rubo; Ki nnkankan ma baa gorii won; Ojo naa ni Wsinsin-Tente ba le won lori; Mo sa pamo, sa pamo; Ori mi loun o sa pamo; Mo rin ni koro, ni koro; Eda mi loun o fe koro; Dia fun Esinsin-Tente; O n torun bo wale aye; Won ni ko rubo; Ki nnkankan ma ba gorii re; O gbe bo, o rubo; O wewo iteni-iteni; O wese iteni-iteni; O wa lanu koto; Orin Awo lo nko; O ni mo wewo, wese; Mo jeun Oba; Emi wewo, wese; Mi o ku mo; Mo wewo, we'se; Mo jeun Oba.

Translation

I will hide; But my Orí says that he does not accept me by hiding me; I walk through the alleys; But my Èdá rejects my foot in the alleys; These were the declaration of Ifá in Ilé; When he comes from Heaven to Earth; He was advised to offer ebo; So that nothing could be placed at the Orí of him; She replied that life was acceptable to her, as it was hers; That day, Eni spread over her Orí; I will hide; But my Orí says that he does not accept me by hiding me; I walk through the alleys; But my Orí says that he does not accept me by

94

hiding me; I walk through the alleys; But my Èdá rejects my foot in the alleys; These were the declaration of Ifá to Eni; When it comes from Heaven to Earth; She was advised to offer ebo; So that nothing could be placed to the Orí of her; She replied that life was just and right as it was; That day, Ìté spread over her Orí; I will hide; But my Orí says that she does not accept me hiding; I walk through the alleys; But my Orí says that he does not accept me by hiding me; I walk through the alleys; But my Èdá rejects my foot in the alleys; These were Ifá's declaration to Ìté; When she comes from Heaven to Earth; She was advised to offer ebo; So that nothing could be placed to the Orí of her; She replied that life was acceptable to her, as it was hers; That day, Apere spread over her Orí; I will hide; But my Orí says that he does not accept me hiding; I walk through the alleys; But my Orí says that he does not accept me hiding; I walk through the alleys; But my Èdá rejects my foot in the alleys; These were the declaration of Ifá for Apere; When she comes from Heaven to Earth; She was advised to offer ebo; So that nothing could be placed to the Orí of her; She replied that life was acceptable to her as she knew; That day, Oba spread over her Orí; I will hide; But my Orí says that he does not accept me hiding; I walk through the alleys; But my Orí says that he does not accept me hiding; I walk through the alleys; But my Èdá rejects my foot in the alleys; These were Ifá's declaration to Oba; When he comes from Heaven to Earth; She was advised to offer ebo; So nothing could be placed on

95

that of him; She replied that life was acceptable to her as she knew; That day, Adé stretched out on him; I will hide; But my Orí says that he does not accept me hiding; I walk through the alleys; But my Orí says that he does not accept me hiding; I walk through the alleys; But my Èdá rejects my foot in the alleys; These were Ifá's declaration to Adé; When he comes from Heaven to Earth; She was advised to offer ebo; So that nothing could be placed to the Orí of her; She replied that life was acceptable to her as she knew; That day, Iye Okin merìndílógún was placed in her Orí; I will hide; But my Orí says that he does not accept me hiding; I walk through the alleys; But my Orí says that he does not accept me by hiding me; I walk through the alleys; But my Èdá rejects my foot in the alleys; These were the Ifá declaration for Iye Okin; When he comes from Heaven to Earth; She was advised to offer ebo; So that nothing could be placed to the Orí of her; She replied that life was acceptable to her as she knew; That day, Esinsin-Tente was placed in her Orí; I will hide; But my Orí says that he does not accept me by hiding me; I walk through the alleys; But my Orí says that he does not accept me hiding; I walk through the alleys; But my Èdá rejects my foot in the alleys; These were the Ifá statement for Esinsin-Tente; When he comes from Heaven to Earth; He was advised to offer ebo; So nothing could be placed on that of him; complied; I washed the bottom of it; Then he opened his mouth; And he began to sing the song of Awo; He says: "I wash my hands and feet"; And the party

96

with Oba; "I wash my hands and feet"; "And party with Oba"; "I wash my hands and feet"; "I will die no more"; "I wash my hands and feet"; "And party with Oba."

PROPHESY

Ifá says that he likes to have attention and recognition at all times. You always get the attention. Ifá advises that we should no longer be complacent with what achievements he had achieved until the zenith of his career in life was reached. However, he must be cautious in his quest for recognition at all times. Ifá says that even though one must try to reach the top, however, he must be cautious in his search. Ifá also says that you should learn the attitudes of the elders and dignitaries in the community. In this way, you will move in the midst of the elders and very important personalities.

BABA EJIOGBE VERSE 11

Osan ni o san pe; Oru ni o ru pe; Oru ni o kan baba m'esin lese pin-pin-pin; Dai fun Yeye eni; Yeye eni ntorun bo wale aye; Yoo waa gbe'ni nigbayi o; Baba eni kii gbe'ni I ti; Dia fun Ori eni; Ori eni ntorun bo waye; Yoo waa gbe'ni nigbayi o; Ori eni kii gbe'ni i ti; Dia fun Ikin eni; Ikin eni ntorin bo waye; Yoo waa gbe'ni nigbayii o; Ikin eni kii gbe'nii ti.

97

Translation

The day cannot last long; And the night can't last long; The night cannot glue extra hooves to a horse's leg; Ifá message for the mother; When it comes from heaven to earth; She will come and support you this time; The mother cannot stop giving a support; Ifa message for one's father; When it comes from heaven to earth; He will come and give you a support of this time; A father cannot stop giving a support; Ifá message for one's Orí; If it comes to raise the earth; He will come and give a support of this time; One's Ori cannot help but support one; Ifá message for Ikin (Ifa) itself; When he came from heaven to earth; Will come and give a support of this time

One's Ikin cannot fail to give support.

PROPHESY

Ifa assures her that everything she undertakes in life she will achieve. It will not be a failure in his life. You have come into this world to be successful and achieve. You are destined to be one of the movers and shakers of this world.

Ifa advises you to offer ebo with two pigeons, two roosters, two hens, two guinea fowl, two rats, two fish and money. After this, it is necessary to feed the Orí of his mother, his father, his Orí and his Ifa. If your parents are dead, feed them like Egúngùn, but if they are alive, let them feed their

Orí.

BABA EJIOGBE VERSE 12

A gbon bi Ako; A go bi Ako; Ako gbongbon-ongbon, Ako
ko wale; Ako googoogo, enikan ko lee gb'Ako ta; Agba to fi
ilee re sile; To n kiri ile onile kiri; Oun laa pe Ako; K'onile o
huwa gbodo; K'onile o se pelepele; Ako o re'le miiran
dandan; A sipa tan, a yanngede; A yanngede, a sipa; Dia fun
Oninààja-Agùnyin; Omo eri kan beri owo je; Omo ori ti
nsunkun ate; Omo bebe-idi ti nsunkun oun o gun ibaaka
lesin; O naja ilekile titi; Bee ni ko rere je o; Won ni ko lo maa
ba Orunmila sowo po; O gbe'bo, o rubo; A kii ba Orunmila
sowo; Keni o ma r'ere aje; Aje ni nba ni peena aya; A kii ba
Orunmila sowo; Keni o ma r'ere aya; Aya ni nba ni peena
omo; A kii ba orunmila sowo; Keni o ma rere omo; Omo
ni nba ni peena ile; A kii ba orunmila sowo; Keni oma rere
ile; Ile ni nba ni peena esin; A kii ba orunmila sowo; Keni
oma ri ere esin; Esin la o maa gun sawo; Ayanmo bi Eji-
Ogbe ko loba nile Ifa; Esin la o maa gun sawo.

Translation

Wisdom is from Ako; The madness belongs to Ako; As wise
as Ako is, he can't go home; As foolish as Ako is, he cannot
be sold into slavery; The old man who came out of his own
house; And he moved over other people's houses; It is the
person named Ako; Let the occupant of the house beware;
Let the occupant of the house of meekness; If the occupant

of the dwelling is not prudent; If the occupant of the house does not show meekness; Ako will surely go away to another house; With arms akimbo, he will majestically match; He walks majestically, arms on hips; These were Ifá declarations for Onináàja-Agùnyin; Descendants of the Orí, who is looking for a cover to match; And from the waist and buttocks of beads in search of a mule to ride like a horse; He got involved in various places is merchandise; But he didn't have the profit as for his efforts; He was advised to associate with Orunmila; He complied and offered the appropriate sacrifice; One cannot enter into association with Orunmila; To not have the benefit of wealth; Wealth is what attracts his spouse; One cannot enter into association with Orunmila; So that one does not have the benefit of children; Spouse is the one who attracts children; One cannot enter into association with Orunmila; So that one does not have the benefit of children; Children are the ones who attract decent accommodation; One cannot enter into association with Orunmila; To not have a decent home; Home is what horses are drawn to; One cannot enter into association with Orunmila; To not have horses.

PROPHESY

Ifá says that he has no other source of support except Òlódúmarè, the Orí and Ifa. It is through Ifa that will give him wealth, success, health and popularity is assured

100

Ifa says that usually as part of his longing for attention and recognition, he will try to show others how smart you are. Ifá says that all his "intelligence" usually exposes his madness. On the contrary, if someone tries to underestimate intelligence, that person will be surprised when he realized from the person how intelligent you really are.

Ifá says, in conclusion, that he will bring the iré of wealth, spouse, children, house, the horse, longevity and good health for you. You have to trust Ifá at all times. There is need d to offer Ebo of Arùkòré. It is advised to offer two pigeons, two hens, two roosters and money. It is also necessary to feed Ifá with four rats, four fish, palm oil and liquor.

BABA EJIOGBE VERSE 13

Sunkere sunkere; Awo Ile lo dia fun Ile; Gbakere gbakere; Awo Ona dia f'Ona; Okurukuru-afedo-wole; Awo Oja lo dia f'Oja; Won ni ki awon meteeta rubo; Ki won baa le di eleni; Ile nikan ni nbe leyin to nsebo; Ko pe, ko jinna; Ile nikan naa lo waa d'eleni; Ile nikan lo rubo apesin.

Translation

To move slowly; The farm Awo made Ifa divination to Ilé; To drag slowly; The Awo of Ona, made Ifá divination for

Ona; Okúrúkúrú-Afedo-wolè; The Awo of the Oja, market, made Ifá divination for Oja; The three of them were advised to offer ebo so that they would have companions; Only Ile, House complied and offered ebo; In a short time, not far away; Only Ile was able to have companions; Only Ile offered the ebo and got the companions.

PROPHESY

Ifá says that you will be blessed with property. Ifa assures you that even if there are difficulties you are facing. You must overcome them all. Ifá says that he has to take the issue of ensuring an adaptation of his own gravity. Ifá also advises him to be warned about how to relate to his brothers. He doesn't give you chance for petty jealousy rivalry and/or envy.

Ifa advises you to offer ebo with two pigeons, two hens, two guinea-fowl, two roosters and money. It is also necessary to feed Ifa with a pig. (But do not let the blood touch Ifa for any reason).

BABA EJIOGBE VERSE 14

A w'Olurojun w'Olurokun; Bee la o r'Olurokun mo; Mo ni nibo l'Olurokun gbe lo; Won ni Olurokun nbe nile aye a w'Aberokun w'Aberokun; Bee la o r'Aberokun mo; Mo ni nibo l'Abrokun gbe lo; Won ni Aberokun nbe lalade Orun; Dia fun Okankanlenirun Irunmole; Won nlo ree fe Aye; Tii somo Olodumare Agotun; Oba ateni ola legelege fori sagbeji; Ebo ni won ni ko waa se.

Translation

We have searched and searched for Olurokun; However, we do not find Olurokun; I asked where Olurokun had gone; They said that Olurokun still in this world; We have searched and searched for Aberokun; However, we do not find Aberokun; I asked him where he had gone to Aberokun; They said that Aberokun is in the heavens; When each of them wanted to proposal and marry Aye; The offspring of Òlódúmarè; Each of them was advised to offer ebo.

PROPHESY

Ifá says that he foresees I will go from the maternity of a sterile woman. This woman is between 30 and 45 years old. The woman in question is too proud. Even though she had never had a child in her life, however, she had been making it difficult for men to focus on a long-term relationship. This woman prefers the casual relationship than a serious relationship.

If she says that this woman should think about having a partner of her own, if she hadn't had any of hers. She has to be less arrogant with her partner and think more seriously about having her own child in her life. If she also says that during the entire period that the woman in question must think seriously about having children, she was busy pursuing worldly possessions.

The woman has to offer Ebo with 200 brown rats, 24 grains that are first tied around her waist and then used as part of the ebo materials. If she already has a round bead tied around her waist, this is the one to use.

Her partner must also offer a brown rat as ebo. These ebo materials will be taken to the outskirts of town and placed alongside the road SEPARATELY. The couple should not go together. The husband should go first, while the wife goes home later, putting her ebo a few meters from her husband's. Ifá says that, if all these are done according to Ifá's specifications, the following year she will meet the woman who will carry the baby herself, either in her womb, ready to deliver, or on her back.

BABA EJIOGBE VERSE 15

Oloooto ti nbe l'aye o p'ogun; Sikasika ibe o mo ni'won egbefa; Ojo lo titi, ko j'oro o dun'ni; Dia fun Orunmila; Oro n dun Akapo; Bee ni ko dun'fa; Ebo ni won ni ko se; O gb'ebo, o ru'bo; Nje Alasuwada parada; Ojumo Onife e mo o; Alasuwada parada; Orunmila parada; Ko o fun mi l'aje, l'aya, l'omo ni're gbogbo; Alasuwada parada; Ewe apada lo ni ki o parada; Koo fun mi ni gbogbo ire ti mo nfe; Alasuwada parada.

Translation

The truthful in the world are not more than 20; The wicked are not less than, 200; Because the matter had taken a long time, the pain of the matter is lessened; They made Ifá divination for Orunmila; When an issue hurts her Akapo; But it doesn't hurt Ifa; She was advised to offer ebo; He complied; Now, Alasuwada, please transform yourself; Onife's day he realized; Alasuwada, please transform; Orunmila, please, transform yourself; And bless me with abundance, spouse, children and I will go in life; Alasuwada, please transform; Alupaida is left authorizing you to transform; And bless me with all the things I'm looking for; Alasuwada, please transform.

PROPHESY

Ifa assures him that he will live his life in comfort. You will not miss anything important in your life. Ifá says that his life was transformed from nothing to everything, from pain to comfort, from necessity to excess and from failure to success. Ifá says that whatever pains he currently has, it does not hurt Ifa at all. That is why it is necessary to offer ebo so that what is giving you pain and anxiety will also be of interest to Ifa.

Ifa advises you to offer ebo with two pigeons, two guinea fowl and money. If this can be done, you will realize that all your wishes will be fulfilled for you, without further delay.

After the ebo had been offered to you, Ifá says that you need to obtain Alupaida leaves, grind them into a fine paste and mix with soap and water for bathing. You also have to tell the truth all the time.

BABA EJIOGBE VERSE 16

Ohun t'enu ba ri; Oun l'enu n je; Dia fun Igbin; Ti yoo j'ile; Ti ko nii ku; Ebo ni won ni ko se; O gb'ebo, o ru'bo; Igbin j'ile e ti ku mo; Igbin j'ile gbogbo omo eni o.

Translation

Whatever the mouth sees: That is what the mouth eats; Ifá message for Igbin, land snail; Who will eat the dust; And he's not going to die; He was advised to offer ebo; She did so; The land snail ate the dust, but escaped death; Did the land snail eat the dust?

PROPHESY

Ifá says that what you eat will never lead to death. You will always be able to escape death caused by food poisoning. Ifá advises to offer ebo with a mature goat (or three roosters) and money.

Born: The Rivers

3.- OGBÈ Ọ̀YÈKÚ

+

O	I
O	I
O	I
O	I

I PRAY:

Ògbè Ọ̀yèkú Bàbá ọmọlú Ogbèato Awo edan A dífá fún iná şe Ikú agba iworo akú kata kata, okó owó lá tinşé ni apé, yangé ọmọ gbogbo eran ko lorugbo Elebo.

IFA DE

- Of the goat
- Transformation and persuasion.
- Overthrow.

PROVERBS

- The Rainbow only occupies the section that God sends
- Whoever wants not to be deceived, not to be deceived
- There is no small man to do evil
- When the mouth does not speak, the words do not offend

BORN:

- The Adanes of the Crown of Òṣùn
- That humans clean their teeth and wash their mouth after food for hygiene and good teeth.
- The virtue of urine. Just as the body eliminates impurities in the urine, you have to get rid of everything bad that surrounds you

BRAND

- Retaliate, Ògbè Ọ̀ yẹ̀ kù will be important by hook or by crook
- Dispossession of positions, be careful not to remove him from the position he holds
- Debts with Òṣùn. She is angry

SIGNALIZE

- Stomach disease.
- Living surrounded by enemies.
- Much envy.

109

- That no spouse accommodates the person.
- Vices.

IFÁ SAYS

- The Òbúko (the person is homeless, has strong sweat, his digestion is slow, he cannot drink many liquids at meals, he likes to eat salads, he is always protesting. He sleeps little, he is nervous).
- From stomach ailments and circulatory problems
- You live surrounded by enemies and envious
- You are looking for a good conjugate and you cannot find
- Of vicious person. Control of sexual debauchery
- Of delicate situations due to deception between family
- The person was not raised by the father
- That the mother does not want the child to marry

PROHIBITIONS

- Do not argue with anyone
- Master your temper so you don't lose

RECOMMENDATIONS

- If you want all your things to go well, attend to the saints and the dead.
- Take care to express a judgment or opinion about a discussion or about something that they ask you so that

you do not harm yourself

- Beware of the father that if he is alive, he can die in terms of one year.
- Beware of justice and cheating in matters of papers

EWÉ ODÙ OGBÈ Ọ̀YÈKÚ

> The leaves of the Sapote tree

PATAKI LISTING

1. The lion the tiger and the goat.
2. The lion the tiger and the coconut.
3. When Oodùa became Olófin's trust.
4. The fall of the king of Ife
5. The persuasion
6. The path of transformation
7. When they wanted to dethrone olófin.
8. This was where the goat rode his mother

WORKS WITH OGBÈ Ọ̀YÈKÚ

WORKS: Secret of the sapote to get things.

Ẹiyelé pints are given to Òsányin, 9 eja tútù keké, leaves and seeds of Sapote, Iyefá prayed, a dry Pitirre of Òsányin, to mount an Iṣé of Òsányin.

The leaves of Sapotes crushed and mixed with ashes kill the Ogu. If the woman's period is abundant, receive the shade of the tree.

Works to eliminate witchcraft taken

To remove the witchcraft from the stomach, for 7 days, cook parsley with Romerillo flowers and sacu-sacu linked with raw milk and otin if it is difficult to get the parsley root and sacu- sacu, use the leaves that are crushed good to get the juice out of it.

Work for health

Ẹbọ is made with Òbúko and Aṣọ funfun, then given to Elégbà Work for when Òṣùn is brave. Debt with Òṣùn

Ẹbọ is made with an Òbúko, Àkúko, they were Malu, an Ìkokò, inso de tigre, adié méjì, òtá méta, a corncob, oyin, eku, eja, epo, omí, Ayanri, ọ̀ pọ̀ lọ̀ pọ̀ owó.

The Òbúko a Òṣùn is decorated with colored ribbons and castrated outside the room, the

corncob is cut into three parts, a stripe is traced with efun on the floor, the cob cut inside the òtá and the oyin, in front of the Ìkokò you put Èṣù, give it an Osaidié and also eyebale the Ìkokò, Òṣùn the Òbúko and adie méjì aperí, the Ìkokò is thrown Iyefá and taken to the closest corner of the house.

Ẹbọ to be well in old age (for Ọkọnrin-okọ̀nrin)

Àkúko Ẹiyelé méjì, toothbrush, 16 pigs, Chinese root, Òbúko, a Lazo, eku, eja, and the secret of the adanes.

For Ọbìrin

Òbúko, adié méjì, Ẹiyelé méjì, a bow, oyin, and other ingredients, ọ̀ pọ̀ lọ̀ pọ̀ owó

work to solve

Òṣùn is given five Zapotes hooked on the Edanes

ẸBỌ:

Àkúko, adié méjì, ẹtu méjì, eran malu, oyin, àgbado, an apron with two pockets, tewéwe, bareta of obí mérindilogun, igba, eku, eja, epo, opolopo owó.

ẸBỌ:

Lerí de malú lerí de Eledé, Àkúko, gbogbo àgbado, gbogbo epo, a pipe (so that he smokes at night and gives off a lot of smoke, so that he defeats death and his enemies), after giving the Àkúko to Elégbà he takes the lerí from Eledé to the river and the one from malú to a hill, if it is for Obìrin it takes adié méjì, ẹiyelé méjì, oyin, 16 pieces of were malú and each one is fitted with a mariwo rod and they are thrown into the igba, he throws oyin at him and stands in front of Òṣùn.

113

ẸBỌ:

Àkúko ẹiyelé méjì, a bell, a small drum dudu, a small drum bata, gbogbo Tenujen, a bottle of otin, one of oyin, eku, eja, àgbado, opolopo owó.

ẸBỌ:

Àkúko, igba okàn, omí tútù, ash, three garabatos, ewé Ifá, laurel, eku, eja, àgbado, opolopo owó.

ẸBỌ:

Àkúko dudu Abeboadie méjì, gio-gio méta, Osaidie okàn, a little chest, obí, aṣọ that he has stored, eko, a crown, a pumpkin, oñigan, malaguidí, ìtanná, eku, eja, àgbado, opolopo owó.

Distribution:

Àkúko Dudu and Abeboadie méjì for Òṣùn Osaidie okàn with their ingredients for Elégbà gio-gio méta with their ingredients for Èṣù.

ẸBỌ:

Àkúko, ẹtu, àgbado, tague of a two-pocket apron, mask, igba, other ingredients, opolopo owó.

114

OGBÈ YÈKÚ PÀTAKI 1 THE LION THE TIGER AND THE GOAT.

Pàtaki

When the Lion, the Tiger and the Goat wanted to govern their people, they agreed that the one who trained the most people would govern. The Lion summoned the people to the plain, the tiger at the foot of a tree, and the Goat to a hill. As the people went to the hill, and the Lion believed that it was a trick of the Tiger, and the Tiger the same as the Lion, so when they met, they destroyed each other, leaving the goat ruling the town.

OGBÈ YÈKÚ PÀTAKI 2 THE LION THE TIGER AND THE COCONUT.

Pàtaki

Tod Quenku (He is the Lion), Ikú (He is the coconut), Ekùn (He is the Tiger), Ikú had a piece of land and he made it and for that place Ikú was the Obá, all the animals got into his house, even the Quenku, Ikú went to claim his position and all the animals turned against him and accorded Otokú to Ẹtu in his cage. Realizing that they are all his araye, he went to the house of Òrúnmìlà who made him ẹbọ, Ẹtu went to the cage with a jícara, with Ekùn who was his friend and

115

defended him, Ẹtu arrived at the cage and did nothing but get close to the On Ekùn's side, when he saw Ikú eating, he asked him what he ate, Ikú told Ẹtu that if he cooked that way, he would save him. Ẹtu said yes and Ekùn moved closer to Quenku's side, and when Quenku saw him, he asked what was going on and Ekùn replied that nothing was wrong, he came closer to hear better and in an oversight Quenku threw himself and tore him apart , when the animals saw what Ekùn had done, they fled the place and Ekùn handed the papers to Ẹtu and demanded that he cook for him from that were, but Ẹtu for his part demanded that he tell the other beasts that they should not bother her to nothing, Ekùn said to the other animals: I'm in charge here, and be careful not to disturb Ẹtu. These obeyed and withdrew from those places.

ẸBỌ:

Aìkóodíde, Ẹtu, Eran, ẹyin, Àgbado, tokéke, an apron with two pockets, 16 Orí bars, an Igba owó la meyo.

OGBÈ YÈKÚ PÀTAKI 3: WHEN OODÙA BECAME OLÓFIN'S TRUST.

Pàtaki

When Oodùa went down to earth, Òrúnmìlà recommended

116

him to make ẹbọ with two goats, 4 aṣé kolá, Aṣọ funfun, ẹiyelé mérin and adie mérin funfun. More Oodùa did not make the ẹbọ and descended on earth. But he did it on Olofin's back. When it rained the water fell on him, and the sun punished him from the dawn.

He couldn't quench his hunger. He unexpectedly returned to Ode Òrùn to see Òrúnmìlà. He asked permission a little late, the authorization to make ẹbọ of the first Osode, and Òrúnmìlà told him: You have to double the ẹbọ, Oodùa accepted. After doing so, he returned to Isalayé and fell again on Olofin's back.

At that time the land was arid, the rain stopped falling, pregnant women gave birth badly, no fruit of the field ripened. Seeing this series of calamities, Olofin sent for an Awó named Gbori Jobi Ogulenu Awó (universal god of destiny and medicine). This one arrived, took the awofaka that Olófin had in his house and untefá Osode nile Olófin, and Ogbè Yèkú sees him, and asks him who is that foreigner that you let live on your back, build him a house and install it decently the house was made by Oodùa himself, when Ogulenu finished the construction, he told Olófin: to maintain this you have to give Oodùa two goats, opolopo funfun, a basket with 101 Igbin, 101 Akará, Oyin, Efún, Epó, opolopo Owó. This was given to Oodùa and so all life was done every time Oodùa visited Isalayé. Then the women

117

began to give birth, it rained and the fruits ripened, tranquility and peace reigned on earth.

OGBÈ YÈKÚ PÀTAKI 4 THE FALL OF THE KING OF IFE

Pàtaki

There was a King in the land of Ifé, who was plunged into an atmosphere of betrayal, by the staff that made up the court. As time passed, the king's situation became more tense, so he became ill. In this town lived an older man, of poor appearance and religious beliefs, this man sensed that he should go in search of a fortune teller, to guide him in fixing his situation. He went to Òrúnmìlà's house, who made Osode for him and this ifá came out, where he told him that great luck was coming to him, something that would completely change his life and that he would become an important and rich man, but for that luck came, I had to do ẹbọ. The man did, and shortly after the ceremony the king of Ifé died.

The people met to elect a new monarch and decided to name that old man who had religious ideas as King. Those who elected him thought that since the new King was many years old, he would not live long, but after taking office the old man enjoyed good health and his government was very beneficial to the people of Ifé and he felt very proud and comfortable. in his leadership activity.

OGBÈ YÈKÚ PÀTAKI 5 THE PERSUASION.

I Pray:

Ogbè Yèkú ni bábà omulo agba Olórun niré demu, agogo nila enu bagba loni ni pa ri koko otenu dundun na lori ni pa ra sidi otenu bata jad Ogbè Yèkú adífáfún Òsányin, Lodafún Òrúnmìlà, Òwònrìn méjì.

Pàtaki

Ogbè Yèkú was the father of the ọmọlú, he was a powerful man and feared by all for a great power, everyone was afraid of him, and he said that whoever stepped on his land would pay with his life.

On his land he had large plantations of timber trees where he hung the skulls of his enemies from those unfortunates who mistakenly entered his land and there was no one who dared to approach.

One day all the inhabitants of Isalayé went to Olofin looking for a solution to this and he sent them to consult ifá. Where Òwònrìn méjì came out, who ordered him to make ẹbọ with musical instruments and take them to the land of Ogbè Yèkú. But there was no one who wanted to do it, to which the daughter of Òwònrìn méjì said, I am going and will master it. The maiden arrived and entered those lands playing the music, and seeing her Ogbè Yèkú said: Stand up beautiful Obìrin, you are very pretty and I do not want to hurt you, to which she replied, I am coming for you and I will take you. He was amazed by the bravery, beauty and music of the daughter of Òwònrìn méjì.

She overpowered him and led him before Olófin and said, furthermore: I will defeat all of you, to which Olófin said, Èṣù was too. He restored it to his land and every time he needs it, you have to look for Òwònrìn méjì to bring it.

OGBÈ YÈKÚ PÀTAKI 6: THE PATH OF TRANSFORMATION

Pàtaki

It was a time when there was a lot of famine in the land and Nifọmọloko had a part of his land planted with Iṣu (Yam), Òrúnmìlà, passing by, took out some Yams and threw them into his Apó, but Nifọmọloko saw him and accused him of thief When justice arrived, Elégbà also arrived who, aware of the problem, told Òrúnmìlà: show justice the content of your Apó, when justice looked, he only saw Ekuteles and

Nifomoloko said: yes, I saw him when he threw the Işu inside his Apó. Now how are mice? It was that Elégbà with his virtue, had transformed the Işu into Ekuteles, Elégbà said: As Nifomoloko has accused Òrúnmìlà of being an innocent thief, since he has not stolen anything, he has to compensate him for the defamation. They continued the lawsuit until they screwed it up.

OGBÈ YÈKÚ PÀTAKI 7: WHEN THEY WANTED TO DETHRONE OLÓFIN.

Pàtaki

In this Odù it was when at the beginning of the World, they wanted to dethrone Olófin and they put Adé (Crown) on him and gave him adie méjì, so that he would hold on to the position and be as he had always been, Orí of all the Òşàs, and respected by all until the end of the world.

OGBÈ YÈKÚ PÀTAKI 8: THIS WAS WHERE THE GOAT MOUNTED HIS MOTHER.

Pàtaki

El Chivo lived in the company of his mother and the time came when he needed to have his wife and one morning before going to work, he told his mother: Let him have a woman for the night and he left her twenty-five pesos. At night when the Goat arrived, he asked her mother about her assignment, and she replied that everything was already arranged. At bedtime he was introduced to his mother, what more woman than me?

And since then, the Goat rides his mother.

4.- TRADITIONAL IFA OGBE OYEKU

OGBE OYEKU VERSE 1

Ogbè Yèku baba àmúlù; Orí ogbó, orí ató ni baba edan; Òsòòrò ni Baba òjò; Díá fún Gbàtólá; A bù fún Gbàtówò; Níjó ti àwon méjèèjì nfomi ojú sùngbéré Ire; Wón ní kí wón rúbo; Wón gb'ébo, wón rúbo.

Translation

Ogbe Yeku is the father of all combinations; Longevity is the father of EDAN; The torrent is the father of the rain; They were the ones who launched Ifá for Gbàtólá; They also launched Ifá for Gbàtówò; When the two were advised to offer sacrifice; They obeyed the advice.

PROPHESY

Ifá says that he foresees the IRE where Ogbè-Òyèkú is

revealed during the Ifá consultation. Ifá says that he foresees the IRE of happiness. Ifá says that the revelation is for two people. The two of them will be happy in their lives. They too will be successful in their lives. Ifá recommends sacrifice for them

Pataki

Gbàtólá and Gbàtówò went to the three Babaláwo mentioned above to inquire about what they needed to do for them to be successful in life. The Babaláwo advised them to offer each one two bottles of pure honey as a sacrifice. They were also asked to offer money as a sacrifice, which they complied with. After this, the Babaláwo prepared appropriate spiritual medicine for the two to use. Soon Gbàtólá and Gbàtówò became very successful. They decided to offer the prescribed sacrifice again then. They were told, however, that it is not practical to offer a sacrifice twice for the same problem and for the same Ifá verse. All they could do is give praise to their Babaláwo for his competition. The Babaláwo will give praise to Ifá on the other hand, give praise to Olódúmarè.

Ogbè Yèku baba àmúlù; Orí Ogbó, Orí ató ni baba edan; Òsòòrò ni Baba òjò; Díá fún Gbàtólá; A bù fún Gbàtówò; Níjó ti àwon méjèèjì nfomi ojú sùngbéré Ire; Wón ní kí wón rúbo; Wón gb'ébo, wón rúbo; Njé ayé ye Gbàtólá; Ayé ye Gbàtówò; Ayé oyin kìí kan.

Translation

Ogbe Yeku is the father of all combinations; Longevity is the father of EDAN; The torrent is the father of the rain; They were the ones who launched Ifá for Gbàtólá; They also launched Ifá for Gbàtówò; When both of them were in need of all the good things in life; They were advised to offer sacrifice; They obeyed advice; Consequently, Gbàtólá's life is successful; Gbàtówò's life is also a success. Honey life is never bitter.

Ifá says that he foresees happiness and success for two people who had come for Ifá consultation.

OGBE OYEKU VERSE 2

Ogbe 'Yèkú baba àmúlù; Orí Ogbó, Orí ató ní baba edan; Òsòòrò ni baba òjò; Sègèrè ló tó ilùú lù; Eyín erin ló tó Obaá fon; Díá fún Kìnnìún arítò gba'jù; Èyí ti yóó maa lé omo eranko geregere; Kárí inú igbó; Wón ní kó rúbo; Ó gbébo, ó rubo.

Translation

Ogbe Yeku is the father of all combinations; Longevity is the father of EDAN; The torrent is the father of the rain; A specialist drummer is the only one capable of beating a drum to produce melody; An Obà is the only one capable of blowing the tusk of the elephant (Ivory); They were ones who cast Ifá for the Lion that urinates around the forest; Who will also be following all the prey around the forest (without killing one); They advised him to offer sacrifice; He complied.

PROPHESY

Ifá tells the person that he will be able to fulfill his mission in life. You will not fail in your efforts in life. You must offer the appropriate sacrifice so that your efforts in life are not wasted.

Pataki

The lion went to consult Ifá when all the things he was doing added up to nothing. He keeps hunting over the forest without killing any. He then went for Ifá consultation to find out whether or not he will be able to accomplish his mission of hunting great profit with ease. The lion was advised to offer sacrifice. What was he going to offer as a sacrifice? Two bottles of liquor and money. The liquor is specially prepared for the lion so that he can drink. He began to drink the liquor. Any time the lion drinks the liquor, he would urinate in a circle round the bush, any prey that entered that urination circle would find it impossible to get out of the ring. This is due to the power of the liquor. The Lion would come and kill the trapped prey within the circle with ease.

Ifá says that the client will be able to achieve the desires of his heart with ease. He must offer sacrifice and must be hopeful in life. He is going to become a powerful person in life.

Ogbe 'Yèkú baba àmúlù; Orí Ogbó, Orí ató ni baba edan; Òsòòrò ni baba òjò; Sègèrè ló tó ilùú lù; Eyín erin ló tó Obaá fon; Díá fún Kìnnìún arítò gba'jù; Èyí ti yóó maa lé omo seanko geregere; Kárí inú igbo; Wón ni kó rúbo; Ó gbébo, or rubo; Kò pé, kò jìnnà; Ire gbogbo wá ya dé tùrtúru.

Translation

Ogbe Yeku is the father of all combinations; Longevity is the father of Edan; The torrent is the father of the rain; A specialist drummer is the only one capable of beating a drum to produce melody; An Obà is the only one capable of blowing the tusk of the elephant; They were ones who cast Ifá for the lion that urinates around the forest; Who was also following all the prey around the forest they advised him to offer sacrifice; He complied. Before long, without much effort; All the good things of life, came in abundance.

Ifá says that the client will be able to achieve his life's ambition and without much trouble as well.

OGBE OYEKU VERSE 3

Ogbe Yeku-Yeku; Díá fún Olófin; Tí ìpín rè yóó maa yè lo.

Translation

Ogbe Yeku- Yeku; I launch Ifá for Olofin; When your good fortunes are running out.

PROPHESY

Ifá says that the client must offer the appropriate sacrifice, to put his destiny on the legitimate foundation. Ifá says that his good luck is leaving. The client is a supportive person, but he must offer the appropriate sacrifice to prevent him from experiencing suffering and ill fate.

Pataki

When Olofin was installed as the Obà, the valued popularity of him was very high. He was extremely wealthy and his subordinates respected, adored and feared him. The town where he was the king (Ilé-Ife) also testifies to great prosperity. Suddenly Ile-Ife wasn't any nicer. Everything started to turn upside down. Matters responded to his penalty, not dwelling on the King's instructions from him. They refused to obey him and refused to bring him his debts. When the situation became unbearable for him, he went and consulted Ifa with Ogbe-Yeku-Yeku.

Ogbe-Yeku then told him that this situation can be remedied. He recommended that 16 rats, 16 fish and money for the sacrifice. He also recommended chickens as a ritual to Ifá. All this Olofin did.

Within three months everything changed for the better in Ile-Ife. Matters became more prosperous than ever before. They showed their appreciation to Olofin as well, giving him more respect than ever before:

Ogbe Yeku-Yeku; Day fun Olofin; Tí ìpín rè yóó maa yè lo; Kíla or fi gbe ìpín dide? Eku, eh; The ó fi gbé ìpín dìde ò; Eku, hey.

Translation

Ogbe Yeku-Yeku; I launch Ifá for Olofin; When his good fortune is running out; What will be used to put destiny on its correct course? Rats and Fish; It is what we will accustom to put destiny in the correct course; Rats and fish.

Ifá says that the client's misfortune will stop and turn into good fortune. Ifá says that clients will not be dishonored and experience hardship for too long. He only needs to offer sacrifice so prescribed.

OGBE OYEKU VERSE 4

Ogbe 'Yeku ni baba àmúlù; Orí Ogbo, orí ató ni baba edan; Òsòòrò ni Baba ójó; Díá fún Òrúnmìlà; Baba nlo gb'Ódù níyàwó wálé.

Translation

Ogbè Yeku is the father of combinations; Longevity is the father of EDAN; The torrent is the father of rain; They were ones who launched Ifá for Òrúnmìlà; When going to take Odù as a wife.

PROPHESY

Ifá says that he foresees the IRE of a good wife for you. The wife will also give birth to many children for you. If she is a woman who had gone for Ifá consultation, in her marriage opportunities, Ifá says that the woman will prosper where she goes. She will be a good wife and she will have many children. The woman will, however, be very jealous and she will not want to see another woman with her husband.

Pataki

Òrúnmìlà committed himself to Odù, when the political day drawn up was near, Òrúnmìlà called the three Babaláwo mentioned above for the consultation of Ifá. He wanted to know if the relationship will be fruitful and he will be a fruitful and a happy one. Ifá said that it was going to be and that Odù would give birth to many good children for the Òrúnmìlà.

For the client, Ifá says that he or she must offer sacrifice. He or she must offer 16 large snails as a ritual to Odù and money as a sacrifice. The woman in question is extremely jealous. Therefore, it is not advisable for a non-Babaláwo to marry her. Apart from this, she will live happily with her husband-to-be and will bring prosperity and good children to her husband:

Ogbe 'Yeku ni baba àmúlù; Orí Ogbo, orí ató ni baba EDAN; Òsòòrò nor Baba ójó; Day fun Òrúnmìlà; Baba nlo gb'Ódù níyàwó wálé; Odu ngbé ówó; Odu n pon eyin; E wá w'omo Odù beer.

Translation

Ogbè Yeku is the father of all combinations; Longevity is the father of EDAN; The torrent is the father of rain; They were ones who launched Ifá for Òrúnmìlà; When he was going to take Odù as his wife; Odù is carrying (children) in his hands; Odù is tying (children) on his back; Look at the children of Odù in multitude.

Ifá says that you must offer sacrifice to achieve happiness and peace in your marriage with the woman of his choice. If the man does not start yet or starts in the regulation of Ifá he must do it before the marriage. The woman cannot marry someone who is not initiated in Ifá.

OGBE OYEKU VERSE 5

Ogbe Yeku ni baba àmúlù; Orí Ogbo, orí ató ni baba edan;
Òsòòrò ni baba ójó; Díá fún Alárá-nsodè; Ti nmójú ekun
sùnráhùn omo.

Translation

Ogbè Yeku is the father of all combinations; Longevity is
the father of EDAN; The torrent is the father of the rain;
They were the ones who launched Ifá for the alara-Nsodè;
When crying due to sterility.

PROPHESY

Ifá says that he provides the client with the IRE of long life
and that of children. The client is currently having problems
having children. He is also having bad dreams. All of these
are caused by his EGBÉ. He must therefore offer sacrifice
and feed his EGBÉ in the form of rituals. Not only that, he
must urgently prepare an urn for his EGBÉ where he can
perform regular rituals to them. This will stop the bad
dreams from him and will also open the door of children for
him.

Pataki

Alárá-Nsodè is the King of llará. He had many wives, but
none of them could get pregnant. He was very sad because
he knew that it would be impossible for him to leave behind

any heir to the throne. He was also experiencing daily nightmares. He therefore went for Ifa consultation. He was informed that he was not only suffering from sterility, but that his EGBÉ was also prepared to take him to heaven. The Babaláwo advised him then, that he have his own grove for the EGBÉ, where this EGBÉ can calm down. Alara-Nsodè wondered grove of EGBÉ? Where can fried akara be used? èkuru, móín-móín, a rooster, palm oil and money, as ritual elements for the EGBÉ. He complied.

In short, all of his wives became pregnant and gave birth to healthy children. His stormy nights stopped and his life changed for the better. He was very happy from that time. The familiar name of him still continued until today.

Ogbe Yeku ni baba àmúlù; Orí Ogbo, orí ató ni baba edan; Òsòòrò ni baba ójó; Díá fún Alárá-nsodè; Ti nmójú ekun sùnráhùn omo; Wón ní kó sákáalè, ebo ní sése; Ó gbebo, or rubo; Kò pé kò jínnà; E wá bá ni láìkú kangiri; Àìkú kangiri làá bá ni lésè Obàrìsà.

Translation

Ogbè Yeku is the father of all combinations; Longevity is the father of EDAN; The torrent is the father of the rain; They launched Ifá for Alara Nsodè; When crying due to sterility; They advised him to offer sacrifice; He complied; Before long, not too far; Look at us enjoying long life; Longevity is what one enjoys with Obàrìsà.

133

Ifá says that the person who consulted Ifá will live a long time and have many children. He must offer sacrifice and perform ritual for his EGBÉ.

OGBE OYEKU VERES 6

Ogbe Yeku ni baba àmúlù; Orí Ogbo, orí ató ni baba edan; Òsòòrò ni baba ójó; Sègèrè ló tó ilu lù; Eyín erin ló tó Obaá fon; Díá fún Ìwé; Tíí somo 'bìnrin àbàtà; Níjó tó fèyínti mójú ekun sùnráhùn omo.

Translation

Ogbè Yeku is the father of all combinations; Longevity is the father of EDAN; The torrent is the father of the rain; A specialist drummer is the only one capable of beating a drum to produce melody; An Obà is the only one capable of flying Ivory; They were ones who launched Ifá for the ÌWÉ, the female Offspring of the swamp, when she was crying because she had no surviving children.

PROPHESY

Ifá also says that she foresees the IRE of children for you. The person should decorate the waist of their children with Lágídígba (Palm Nuts) beads so that they live long.

Ifá says that the person must offer sacrifice and they will

have many children in life. Ifá says that the person may also be having problems in their projects in life. Projects may be dying or shutting down before they are gone. The client must offer sacrifice and everything will be fine again.

Pataki

ÌWÉ's problem was that whenever she delivered a baby, the baby would die shortly after birth. This was happening repeatedly. Therefore, she went to consult Ifa. She wondered what she should do, to put an end to the problem of losing her children at her early ages? What must she do, to have children who would give her a suitable burial, when she joins her ancestors? Those were the questions that ran through her mind.

The five Babaláwo above, advised him to offer sacrifice of four rats, four fish, a hen and money. She must also offer a ritual to Ifá. The ritual elements are, a hen and money. She complied. She was then advised to put Lágídígba which is decorated with beads around the waist of her children, as a protection charm, after they were born. She also complied.

Shortly after, she became pregnant and began giving birth to children. She ensured, however, that the beads were always on the children's waist. "Whoever wants to offer sacrifice, Èsù Òdàrà protects." Whenever the spirit responsible for the death of the previous children comes to take them away again, Èsù Òdàrà would intervene, confusing the spirit. He

135

draws the spirit's attention to the beads and asks, if he knew the implication of such slaughter, anyone in such a situation, adorned with beads. The spirit replied in the negative. Then Èsù Òdàrà said that the spirit that those children have, were superior spirits and if that spirit moves near them, it means that the spirit would be reaping disaster for itself. On hearing this, the spirit withdrew and never returned.

Thus, it was, how all the children of ÌWÉ lived to old age. She was so happy and was praising her Babaláwo like this:

Ogbe Yeku ni baba àmúlù; Orí Ogbo, oríató ni baba edan; Òsòòrò ni baba ójó; Sègèrè ló to ilu lù; Eyín erin ló tó Obaá fon; Day fún Ìwé; Tíí we are 'bìnrin àbàtà; Níjó tó fèyínti mójú ekun sùnráhùn omo; Wón ní kó sákáalè, ebo ní sése; Ó gbebo, or rúbo; Njé lèsí ìí bímo bí Ìwé o? E womo werewere lowo Èrìgì-àlò.

Translation

Ogbè Yeku is the father of all combinations; Longevity is the father of EDAN; The torrent is the father of the rain; A specialist drummer is the only one capable of beating a drum to produce melody; An Obà is the only one capable of flying Ivory; They were ones who launched Ifá for the ÌWÉ, the female Offspring of the swamp, when she was crying because she had no surviving child; She was advised to offer sacrifice; She complied. Now, who is the one who has many children like Ìwé; Look at a multitude of children with Èrìgì-

136

Àlò.

Ifá says that the person must offer sacrifice and he or she will have many children in life. Ifá says that the person may also be having problems in his projects in life. Projects may be dying by shutting down before they are gone. The client must offer sacrifice and all will turn out well for him or her.

OGBE OYEKU VERSE 7

Ogbe Yeku ni baba àmúlù; Orí Ogbó, orí ató ni baba edan; Òsòòrò ni baba ójó; Díá fún Àrànisàn; To n mójú ekun sùnráhùn tomo.

Translation

Ogbè Yeku is the father of all combinations; Longevity is the father of EDAN; The torrent is the father of the rain; They are some that Ifá launched for ARANISAN; When he was crying due to the lack of children.

PROPHESY

Ifá says it foresees IRE from many children to the person for whom Ogbe-Yeku is released. Ifá asks him to offer sacrifice and perform a ritual to EGBÉ. Ifá says that there is someone suffering from sterility. The person will give birth if the proper sacrifice is made.

Pataki

Àrànìsàn went for the Ifá consultation, to find out what he needed, to solve his childlessness problem. He had many wives and they had been living with him for many years. None had been pregnant. The Babaláwo advised him to offer sacrifice and perform rituals for EGBÉ. The sacrifice was, a chicken and money. Ritual materials for EGBÉ - the Àkàrà, èkuru, èko móínmóín, èfó tètè and money. He complied.

Soon after, all the wives of àrànìsàn became pregnant and they gave birth to healthy babies. Àrànìsàn was very happy afterwards:

Ogbe Yeku ni baba àmúlù; Orí Ogbó, orí ató ni baba edan; Òsòòrò ni baba ójó; Day fún Àrànìsàn; To n mójú ekun sùnráhùn tomo. Won ni kó sákáalè, ebo ni sise; Ó gbebo, or rúbo; Kó pé Kò jìnna; E wá bá wa ní jèbútú omo.

Translation

Ogbè Yeku is the father of all combinations; Longevity is the father of Edan; The torrent is the father of the rain; They are some who launched Ifá for Aàrànìsàn; When crying due to the lack of children. They advised him to offer sacrifice.

Ifá says that you should be supported and trusted, you will have many children in life and you will not die as a sterile person.

OGBE OYEKU VERSE 8

Ogbe Yeku le dá; Ti e kó òyèe rè lórí; Díá fún Òrúnmìlà; Ifá nbe ní ràngun òtá; Ifá jí, Ifá n fojoojúmó kominú ogun.

Translation

Ogbe Yeku was he that which released (for you); And you have the ÌYÈRÒSÙN powdered on your head; That was the person who launched Ifá for the Òrúnmìlà; When he (Òrúnmìlà) was in the midst of the enemies; Ifá woke up (early in the morning) and was contemplating; how to contain preventing war.

PROPHESY

Ifá says that there is someone who is correct in the midst of the adversary. The person is surrounded by enemies who do not wish him well. Ifá says that he must offer sacrifice and he will overcome his enemies.

Pataki

Òrúnmìlà was the one who had been followed by his enemies. They planned to ambush him and kill him if possible. He slept one day and had a dream. In the dream, he saw that his enemies were plotting evil against him because of his good deeds. For example, if a person was

139

getting in trouble for witches, he would give the person protection against such people. Ifá a person was sick, he would cure him. Ifá a person wanted to go somewhere and the day would not be favorable, he would warn the client in advance. All of these did not go down well with their neighbors who were the brains behind their problems being found out by the victims. They therefore conspired against Òrúnmìlà and planned to eliminate him or at least, banish him. Òrúnmìlà invited one of his students then "Ogbe-Yeku dá le, Tí e kó òyèe rè lori" to come and consult Ifá him. They told him that he would defeat his enemies. He did need to offer sacrifice and perform rituals, however. Sacrifice: three roosters, three black doves and money. This he persecuted to perform rituals to Ifá and Ògún. For Ifá: - eight rats, eight fish and a guinea-fowl. For Ogun: - a rooster, palm wine, roasted yams, roasted corn, palm oil, liquor, kola nut, and bitter kola. Òrúnmìlà I comply.

The day the enemies were planning to stalk Òrúnmìlà, an argument arose as to what would be better to handle the situation later. The argument degenerated into a big fight and all the weapons that they planned to use against Òrúnmìlà were used against others. That was how Òrúnmìlà above his enemies. He began to sing and dance along with everyone in his house:

Ogbe Yeku gives him; Ti e kó òyèe rè lórí; Day fun Òrúnmìlà; Ifá nbe ní ràngun òtá; Ifá jí, Ifá n fojoojúmó

140

kominú ogun; Wón ní kó sákáalè, ebo ní sése; Ó gbebo, or rúbo; Kò pé, Kò jìnnà; E wá bá ni lárùúsé ogun; Ajàse ogun làwá wá.

Translation

Ogbe Yeku was he that was released (for you); And you have the ÌYÈRÒSÙN powdered on his head; That was the person who launched Ifá for Òrúnmìlà; When he was in the midst of enemies; Ifá woke up and was contemplating how to contain the war by preventing; They advised him to offer sacrifice; He complied. Before long, not too far; Look at us celebrating victory over the adversary.

Ifá says that you will overcome all your opponents. You must offer sacrifice and you must feed Ifá and Ògún, so that the two of them protect you and break the conspiracy of your enemies.

OGBE OYEKU VERSE 9

Ogbe Yeku baba àmúlù; Orí Ogbó, orí ató ni baba edan; Òsòòrò ni baba ójó; Díá fún Olúkòso làlú; Omo a gb'Egùn ma fò; Omo f'Ota werewere ségun; Omo a firì wòòwòò sétè; Nigba tó n be láàrin àgbátèmó ogun araye.

Translation

Ogbè Yeku is the father of all combinations; Longevity is the father of Edan; The torrent is the father of the rain; They

141

are some that launched Ifá for lalu de Olúkòso; Offspring of him who understands Eegun's language perfectly, but refuses to speak it. Offspring of him who uses enough pebbles to conquer enemies; Offspring of him who uses dew drop to disperse conspiracy; When in the midst of the conspiracy of the enemies of him.

PROPHESY

Ifá also foresees I will go for victory over the adversary. You are surrounded by many treacherous people, but you will definitely overcome your enemies. You need to offer the appropriate sacrifice to facilitate a quick victory for your opponents.

Pataki

Shangó was the person against whom his enemies were conspiring. They planned to destroy him and all his might. Shangó then went for the consultation of Ifá. They told him that he would overcome his enemies. They advised him to offer sacrifice. The sacrifice: - three roosters, a ram, 200 pebbles and a mortar. The mortar would turn the pebble upside down and place it in the base of the mortar, a Shango stone ax would be placed in the middle of the base of the mortar. Everything would then be put in the open air for seven days.

All this was done by Shangó and on the eighth day, while the enemies gathered to leave the gate of their plot, thunder struck in the middle of it, many of them died and those who survived scattered in disorder and panic. The survivors secretly went to Shango, to deny their individual and collective participation in any conspiracy against him in life.

This is how Shango overcame his enemies. He was singing and he was dancing:

Ogbe Yeku baba àmúlù; Orí Ogbó, orí ató ni baba edan; Òsòòrò ni baba ójó; Day fún Olúkòso làlú; Omo a gb'Egùn ma fò; Omo f'Ota werewere segun; Omo a firì wòòwòò sétè; Nigba tó n be láàrin àgbátèmó ogun araye. Wón ni kó take him out, ebo ni sise; Ó gbebo, or rúbo; Kò pé, Kò jìnnà; E wá bá ni láruúsè ogun; Ajàsé ogun làwá wà; Njé heel n peri Oba or? to! Èmi ò perìí re Àlàdó!

Translation

Ogbè Yeku is the father of all combinations; Longevity is the father of Edan; The torrent is the father of the rain; They are some who launched Ifá for the lalu of Olúkòso; Offspring of him who understands Eegun's language perfectly, but refuses to speak it. Offspring of him who uses enough pebbles to conquer enemies; Offspring of him who uses dew drops to disperse conspiracy.

143

OGBE OYEKU VERSE 10

Ogbe Yeku baba àmúlù; Orí Ogbó, orí ató ni baba edan;
Òsòòrò ni baba ójó; Díá fún Oba lálàde Òyó; Olá, oko
aya'ba Lágbo; Wón ní Odùn nìí l'odún olàa reé pé.

Translation

Ogbè Yeku is the father of all combinations

Longevity is the father of rain; The torrent is the father of
the rain

They are some who launched Ifá for the King of Òyó; The
honourable, husband of the King many wives; They told
him that he will be prosperous this year.

PROPHESY

Ifá says that it foresees an iré of prosperity, you will prosper
in all your commercial tasks. Ifá says that this year is your
year of prosperity. Your business will boom before the year
is out. You must offer sacrifice and perform ritual for your
Orí.

Pataki

The King of Oyo (Añaafin) took up residence early in his
life. His business did not move well. He was very poor. This
was the main cause of caring for him, before he went for Ifa
consultation. They asked him to offer two sheep. One as a

sacrifice and the other for the ritual to his Orí. Ten meters of linen materials. Out of this, a complete set of Agbada (ordinary dress) will be made dansiki and pants to be made for him with white cap. For a woman, a full dress with head-bow. He must also put on a pair of white shoes, and sit on a new mat, when the Orí ritual is performed. (The client will also offer enough money as a sacrifice and retribution for the ritual performance).

They also advised him that on the day his Ori feeds, he should not go out anywhere, throughout that day. He was also told that he should not lock his door, because when the spirits in charge of prosperity come, they must not be locked out of the house. To all this, he obeyed.

Before the year ended, the spirits in charge of success and prosperity visited him several times, they found his door open and entered his house. He became very wealthy. He was very pleased.

Ifá says the person for whom this Odù is revealed, must offer sacrifice as previously prescribed, he must also perform rituals to his Orí. He must not lock his door, during the period that he offers his sacrifice. On the day of the ritual, he must not go anywhere and must dress completely in white. He will be prosperous before the end of the year.

Ogbe Yeku baba àmúlù; Orí Ogbó, orí átó ni baba edan; Òsòòrò ni baba ójó; Díá fún Oba lálàde Òyó; Olá, oko aya'ba Lágbo; Wón ní Odùn nìí l'odún olàa reé pé. Wón ni kó take him out, ebo ni sise; Ó gbebo, or rúbo; Kò pé, Kò jìnnà; Ire Ajé wá ya dé tùrtúru.

Translation

Ogbè Yeku is the father of all combinations; Longevity is the father of edan; The torrent is the father of the rain; They are some who launched Ifá for the King of Òyó; The honourable, husband of the King many wives; They told him that he will be prosperous this year. They advised him to offer sacrifice; He complied. Before long, not too far; The IRE of wealth came in abundantly.

Ifá says that the person for whom this Odù is revealed will be successful in life. He will also hold a leadership position in his life. He must not lose hope if there is any penalty now. Everything will work to his advantage.

OGBE OYEKU VERSE 11

Ogbe Yeku baba àmúlù; Orí Ogbó, orí ató ni baba edan; Òsòòrò ni baba ójó; Díá fún Òòsà-Nlá Òsèèrèmàgbò; Ti n mójú ekun sùnráhùn ire gbogbo.

Translation

Ogbè Yeku is the father of all combinations; Longevity is

146

the father of Edan; The torrent is the father of rain; They are some who launched Ifá for Òòsà-Nlá Òèèrèmàgbò; When in need of IRE for the finer things in life.

PROPHESY

Ifá says that he foresees IRE in all aspects of his life. Ifá says that nothing will be lacking in his life - wealth, children, legitimate land, long life and so on. If the situation is now tough, it is only fair to have a little patience. Before long all your problems will be solved and the door of good fortune will open for you. You just need to offer the appropriate sacrifice and perform a ritual for Obàtálá.

Pataki

When Obàtálá was in trouble, he consulted the three Babaláwo mentioned above. All his efforts in life added up to zero. He wanted to know what to do in order to achieve global success in life.

Obàtálá was advised to offer sacrifice of four guine-birds, four pigeons and money. He complied. Before long, everything became normal and he was successful in life.

In addition to the sacrifice offered by Obàtálá, you must also perform a ritual to Obàtálá for the client. Ritual materials: - four snails, native chalk, white kola nut, bitter kola and money. Ifá says that life will be according to the client and

147

you will not lack anything in life.

Ogbe Yeku baba àmúlù; Orí Ogbó, orí ató ni baba edan; Òsòòrò ni baba ójó; Díá fún Òòsà-Nlá Òsèèrèmàgbò; Ti n mójú ekun sùnráhùn ire gbogbo. Wón ní kó sákáalè, ebo ní sése; Ó gbebo, or rúbo; Kò pé, Kò jìnnà; Ká wá bá ni bá jèbútú ire gbogbo.

Translation

Ogbè Yeku is the father of all combinations; Longevity is the father of EDAN; The torrent is the father of rain; They were ones who launched Ifá for Òòsà-Nlá Òèèrèmàgbò; When in need of IRE for the finer things in life. They advised him to offer sacrifice, he complied. Before a long time, not too far; See us in the midst of abundant well-being.

Ifá says that life will be interesting and rewarding for you.

OGBE OYEKU VERSE 12

Ogbe Yeku baba àmúlù; Orí Ogbó, orí ató ni baba edan; Òsòòrò ni baba ójó; E jé ká wo ibi Ire; Ká té ení eni Ire sí; E jé ká wo ibi Ire; Ká fi ìdí òrèrè balè; Díá fún Òrúnmìlà; Gbogbo òtòòkùlú wón láwon ó bá'fá se mó.

Translation

Ogbè Yeku is the father of all combinations; Longevity is

the father of EDAN; The torrent is the father of the rain; Let us find a good place; To put the mat for a good person; Let us find a good site; To put the staff of the Òrèrè; They were ones who launched Ifá for Òrúnmìlà; When all the important dignitaries resolved to have nothing to do with him again.

PROPHESY

In Ogbe-Yeku, Ifá says that he foresees an iré of prosperity, an iré of victory over the adversary and an iré of love for people. Many people will love it. In the present you are conspiring against yourself. They are plotting against you. With proper sacrifice, all those who conspired against you will gather around you.

Pataki

Òrúnmìlà was the person who was conspiring against those who had been close allies of him until now. None of them wanted to have anything to do with him again. He therefore went to the Babaláwo mentioned above. The Odù that was revealed when Ifá was released was, Ogbe-Oyeku. Òrúnmìlà was advised to offer sacrifice. The material sacrifice: -two pigeons. They also asked him to perform ritual to Ifá. Ritual material: - a guinea-fowl and money. He complied. A special soap consisting of the following was prepared for him:

Sìkírínmidìn leaves, sulfur, common flies enough.

149

Everything was pounded together and mixed with soap. They then asked her to use his bare hand to remove the amber from the fire and grind it into powder. He complied. Then the powder is used to print Ogbe-Oyeku. The Odù was recited as an incantation. Soon, all the people who didn't want to see him before couldn't do without him. They all loved him more than ever before. He became happy and was dancing, singing and reciting the Odù daily:

Ogbe Yeku baba àmúlù; Orí Ogbó, orí ató ni baba edan; Òsòòrò ni baba ójó; E jé ká wo ibi Ire; Ká tea ení eni I will go yes; E jé ká wo ibi Ire; Ká fììdí òrèrè balè; Day fun Òrúnmìlà; Gbogbo òtòòkùlú wón láwon ó bá'fá se mó; Ifá ló ní kí e wáá féràn mi; Àféká layé n fé iná; Ifá ló ní kí e wáá féràn mi; Àlàjáyé loorun n ràn; Ifá ló ní kí e wáá féràn mi; Esinsin kìí mó ní kó too fowo Ire ba'ni; Ifá ló ní kí e wáá féràn mi; Sìnkínrínmidìn, a fàì moni kóni móra.

Translation

Ogbe Yeku is the father of all Ifá combinations; Longevity is the father of Edan; The torrent is the father of the rain; Let us find a good place; To set your sights on a good place; To put the mat for a good person; Let us find a good site; To put the Orere staff; They were ones who launched Ifá for Òrúnmìlà; When all the important dignitaries resolved to have nothing to do with him again; Ifá is he who says you must all love me; When Fire is blown, it spreads around; Ifá is he who says you must all love me; When the sun shines, its rays reach every part of the world. Ifá is he who says you must all love me; The housefly doesn't need to know one before touching one with its good hands; Ifá is he who says you must all love me; Sìnkírínmidìn does not know one before throwing one on himself.

For a client who had come for Ifá consultation, if this Odù is revealed, the client should be warned to do things against his friends that may turn against him. However, if he had already been doing so, he is advised to offer the sacrifice, perform the rituals and use the special soap prescribed above. Within a week or two, everything will return to normal for him.

OGBE OYEKU VERSE 13

Gberi gan; Díá fún Egbin Orentele Olorun-un jolo; Níjó to n ló sí awujo egbe; Wón ní kí ó má ló; Kí ó sí rúbo ija óogun; Ó gbebo, ó rúbo.

Translation

Gberi gan; He was the one who launched Ifa for Egbin the only proportionate and healthy neck. Going to attend his society function; They advised him not to attend; They also asked him to offer sacrifice against those who planned to fight him with evil charms; He obeyed both advice.

PROPHESY

Ogbe-Yeku says that the person should be very careful in the midst of his friends. If he is a member of an Association, club, or society, he must refrain from attending any functions of the association, club, or society for some time. This is because he is a very active member of this society, but other members are envious of his contributions and achievements, inside and outside the association, club or society. Therefore, they are planning evil against you.

Ifá also says that you recently had a dream that gave you a premonition about what could happen to you in that association of friends. He must take the dream seriously. However, with the proper sacrifice, the evil plans of his colleagues will turn against them.

Pataki

Egbin is considered to be the prettiest and most graceful among the antelope family. He was a member of the animal society and he was very vocal during any of his deliberations. In addition to this, he was also very successful in his business endeavors. He attended meetings in his best dress. This action made the tortoise, the monkey, the deer, the leopard and so on become envious of Egbin. They considered that he was very proud and in tune. They started to be against him, because he planned to move the Lion as King. They all started plotting against him. They were however aware of the fact that he was very influential. For that reason, they reasoned that it would be unwise to physically attack him. Therefore, they planned to put an evil charm, which will destroy his skin and make him ugly on his chair, so that if he sat on the chair, he would become leprous. Then they would take that excuse, to expel him from society. These evil conspirators decided to go and find the Pangolin who was a botanist renowned for evil charms. So, he prepared the charm for them and they always rubbed it on the chair specifically reserved for Egbin.

The night before the day of the society meeting, however, Egbin had a bad dream. In the dream, he saw himself hunted away, chained hand and leg through other animals. When he woke up, the dream greatly disturbed him. Therefore, he went to a Babaláwo known as Gbérí gan, early in the morning, in search of Ifá consultation. Ogbe-Yeku was revealed. Gbérí gan told Egbin that he was planning to go somewhere. He told Egbin that he should not go and should not attend any group functions for approximately six months. He also advised Egbin to offer sacrifice of three roosters and money. He must also perform ritual to Èsù Òdàrà with a rooster, two bottles of palm-oil, four kola nuts with three valves (Ventalla) each and money. He complied. Later in the day, all the other animals were present at the meeting, all waiting for Egbin. The special chair prepared for Egbin was put in an eminent place for him to sit in front of.

153

Everyone waiting for Egbin, but he didn't show up. As it was getting late, the conspirators became agitated. They then sent the tortoise to Egbin's house, to persuade him to attend the meeting. The tortoise went to Egbin's house and asked her to come to the meeting.

Egbin pretended to be ill and told the tortoise that his illness would not allow him to attend. The tortoise then told Egbin that he should attend because Egbin was going to be honored especially by other animals and that Egbin should not miss this opportunity. But unfortunately for the tortoise, Egbin refused to attend, suddenly considering Babaláwo's warning.

Meanwhile, other animals that had been waiting for the tortoise began to have second thoughts. Èsù Òdàrà entered their minds and they began to suspect the tortoise, before she came back.

Some of them even said that it was probably, that the tortoise must have gone to Egbin's house to warn him against attending the meeting. They also believed that the tortoise must have received satisfaction from Egbin. The other animals therefore resolved to deal with the tortoise once she returned without Egbin.

When the tortoise returned without Egbin, an argument ensued. The argument later degenerated into a free fight between everyone. In the process, the tortoise's nose was

154

bitten out of the shell, the monkey's buttocks were rubbed against the invention and all the hair was blown away, Pangolin spread the rest of the charm and much landed on the leopard, which produced spots on the body of leopards. The animals scattered in disorder. When Egbin heard about the result of the meeting, he was in favor full of joy and praising the Babaláwo of him.

Gberi gan; Day fún Egbin Orentele Olorun-un jolo; Níjó to n ló yes awujo egbe; Wón ni kí or má ló; Kí ó si rúbo ija óogun; Ó gbebo, or rúbo; Kò pé, kó jìnnà; Ewa wo riru ebo bii tii gbe'ni.

Translation

Gberi gan; He was the one who launched Ifa for Egbin the only proportionate and healthy neck. Going to attend his society function; They advised him not to attend; They also asked him to offer sacrifice against those who planned to fight him with evil Charms; He obeyed both advice. Before long not too far; See how rewarding it is to consider the advice to offer sacrifice.

This was how Egbin overcame his enemies. Ifá says that the client will overcome his enemies. All his bad plans will add up to zero. They will harm us with his bad plans instead of hurting the customer. Offer sacrifice and perform ritual.

OGBE OYEKU VERSE 14

Erù gale; Díá fún Onídè nínú egbin; Níjó tó n lo òde òru; Wón ní kó má lo; Wón ní kó fi aso rè rúbo nítorí ikú sínnsínní; Ó pe Ifá lékèé; Ó pe Èsù lólè.

Translation

Èrù gale; He launched Ifá for Onídè among the antelopes; Going out in the dark; They asked him not to go; They also asked him to offer sacrifice to avoid shoddy death; He called Ifá a swindler; He labeled Èsù a thief.

PROPHESY

Ifá says that the person for whom this Odù is revealed, that he should never be going out at night. Ifá says if you have that habit, you can be badly hurt or even lose your life. You should not wear dark colored dresses. The color is against his being. You will always attract negative spirits towards you. Colors like black, blue-black, chocolate, dark gray and navy blue are not good for you.

Pataki

Onídè was planning to go on a night excursion. He went for the consultation of Ifá in the house of his Babaláwo of him, wind of Erú. They asked him not to go, so that he would not shoot himself with an arrow. They also asked him to offer a sacrifice of a bearded goat, three arrows (today made

156

from twigs), 50 kola nuts, 50 bitter-kola, two bottles of palm-oil, and money. They also asked him to wear the black cloth on it, as a ritual for the Èsù. He abruptly refused. He said that Erù-gàlè was a thief who seeks relief to eat and that there was no difference between Erù-gàlè the Babaláwo and Èsù Òdàrà who wanted the beautiful black dress from him. He angrily left Babaláwo's house and retired.

When the night came, he was fatal. Meanwhile, a hunter had been hunting in the forest without success. Èsù Òdàrà directed the hunter's mind then towards the direction of Onídè.

When the hunter saw the black dress on Onídè, he drew his arrow aimed at Onídè and released the shot. He hit Onídè in the right eye, ending up in the left eye, piercing his brain. Onídè died instantly.

Ifá tells him that he should not doubt the values before offering the sacrifice or performing rituals as prescribed, so that he does not lose his life. This is a very serious aspect of the Odù.

Erù gale; Díá fún Onídè ninú egbin; Níjó tó n lo òde òru; Won ni kó ma lo; Won ni; ó fi aso rè rúbo nítorí ikú Sínnsínní; Ó pe Ifá lékèé; Ó pe Èsù lólè; Ìpín àsebo; Ègbà àitèrù; Òfèrèfèrè; E ò`ríná Ifá kàn jó won o; Òfèrèfèrè.

157

Translation

Èrù gale; He launched Ifá for Onídè among the antelopes; Going out in the dark; They asked him not to go; They also asked him to offer his dark clothes as a sacrifice to avoid shoddy death; He labeled Ifá a swindler; He called Èsù a thief; The consequence of his refusal to offer sacrifice; The result of his refusal to perform rituals; Fiercely; Look how the fire is burning them; Furiously in fact.

Ifá warns against unnecessary obstinacy, lack of confidence and prudence. Please be guided correctly.

OGBE OYEKU VERSE 15

Ogbe Yèréyèré; Díá fún Oya; Tí nlo sí igò eèsùú; Wón ní kó má lo; Kó sí rúbo sí laìkú araa re; Ó pe Awo ní èké; Ó pe Èsù lólè.

Translation

Ogbe Yèréyèré; He launched Ifá for the Lawnmower; Going to the meadow to reside; They advised him not to go; They also asked him to offer the sacrifice to prolong his life; She called her Babaláwo a swindler; She called Èsù a thief.

PROPHESY

Ifá says that the person who is prohibited from leaving or

158

continuing to travel. You should find out beforehand and know the place and the period when you are prohibited from going there. This is because the journey is fraught with danger.

Ifá also says that the person should not venture to change his place of residence or change his job, place of training, factory or where he goes shopping, educational institute in that period. Any change of situation in that period is not advisable.

Pataki

The lawnmower was planning to go and prepare his residence in the meadow. He was advised against doing that. He was also asked to offer sacrifice of three staves, three bundles of dry grass, three roosters and money. He was also advised to offer a rooster and a bottle of palm oil to Èsù as a ritual. She refused to comply and abused the Babaláwo, calling him a thief. She went to the meadow together with all her children. They made their home there. As the dry season approached, however, all the grasses became dry. People living around the neighborhood set the lawns on fire in search of game. The lawn mower and all his children were scattered everywhere and the hunters killed them all with sticks. This is how the lawnmower and all his children lost lives, due to stubborn lawnmowers.

Ogbe Yèréyèré; Day Fun Oya; Tí nlo yes igò eèsùú; Won ni

kó ma lo; Kó si rúbo yes laìkú araa re; Ó pe Awo ní èké; Ó
pe Èsù lólè; Èro Ìpoàti t'Òfà; Enií gbebo nibè kó sebo or.

Translation

Ogbe Yèréyèré; He launched Ifá for the Lawnmower; Going
to the meadow to reside; They advised him not to go; They
also asked him to offer the sacrifice to prolong her life; She
called the Babaláwo her a swindler; She called Èsù a thief.
Travelers to the Ìpo and Ofa villages; Those who are advised
to offer sacrifice, let them do so.

Ifá says that he must offer the prescribed sacrifice and also
consider the warning, so that it is not his fault.

OGBE OYEKU VERSE 16

Èèpo èpà a fara rindinrindin; Díá fún esè kan soso Ogbe; Tó
n loo ye òkú Oloku wó; Wón ní kó má lo; Wón ní kó sì rúbo
àkóbá.

Translation

The shell of the tigernut, with a rectangular shape, was the
one that launched Ifá for one of Ogbe's legs; When going to
see the corpse of other people; They advised him not to go;
They also asked him to offer the sacrifice to avoid getting
involved.

160

PROPHESY

Ifá says that you should not go where a person had simply died. He should not attend the funeral ceremony of a person who has recently died. He may attend the final burial ceremony of someone who has died during the month, whose burial was postponed, however, the important thing is that you must not see a fresh corpse.

Ifá also says that when someone is sick, you should not apply medicine to that person. Because the chances of the person dying from being sick are high, if you apply the medication, everyone can conclude that you were responsible. The fact is, you shouldn't see fresh corpses and you shouldn't apply medication to sick people. It is impossible for anyone born in the odu Ogbe-yeku to enter the medical profession as a Doctor, Nursing Pharmacy, Midwifery, radiology, pathology, etc., or even work in any hospital.

Pataki

One leg of Ogbe had a friend who was very ill. He (Ogbe) was a trained medical botanist. He was then invited by the relations of his ill friend. He went for Ifa consultation before proceeding. His Babaláwo advised him not to go. He was also advised to offer a sacrifice of a rooster and money, to avoid getting involved. He offered the sacrifice and testified at home.

Sick friend relations sent another message to Ogbe. This time he considered the call he applied medication on his friend and the friend died.

He was also called by some other people, to attend to his sick relationship and they all died. We all began to think that it was Ogbe who killed sick people. They all went to his house early one day and dragged him before the Oba.

He tried to explain that he had no responsibility for the deaths of sick people, but no one was ready to listen. The Oba then told him that all available evidence pointed to the fact that Ogbe was the one who killed his patients. Ogbe was banished from the community and was never authorized to practice as a medical botanist again.

Ifá says that the client must not only offer the prescribed ritual, but must also make sure to consider the warning not to get involved in a case that he knows nothing about. Certainly, spirits are against his performance in the field doctor, paramedic. The client must consider this warning, above all, those who are born by this Odù and those to whom this Odù is revealed during the Ìtelódù (initiation) of the Ifá ceremony. If he is Babaláwo, he must not practice herbal medicine at all. He must deal with other aspects of Ifa.

Èèpo èpà to fara rindinrindin; Díá fun esè kan bland Ogbe; Tó n loo ye òkú Oloku wó; Won ni kó ma lo; Wón ní kó sì

162

rúbo àkóbá; Ó rubo; Kò si pa ìkìlò mó; Ogbe ìwo loò seni;
Ogbe ìwo loò seniyàn; Ó ti se n yè kú olókùú wò kiri?

Translation

The shell of the tigernut, with a rectangular shape, was the
one that launched Ifá for one of Ogbe's legs; He was going
to see the corpse of other people; They advised him not to
go; They also asked him to offer the sacrifice to avoid being
implicated. He offered the sacrifice; But he didn't heed the
warning; Ogbe, you are the bad person; Ogbe, you are an
inconsiderate person; Why are you seeing the corpse of
other people around you? It is important for you to observe
these Ifá warnings at all times and to make the sacrifice and
maintain attention.

5- VOCABULARY AND DEFINITIONS

WHAT FOR PROFESSIONAL ETHICS, EVERYTHING MUST KNOW BABALAWO

1. From memory, a large part of the Ifá literary corpus.
a. Masterfully manipulate the instruments of the oracle of divination.
2. Must be a well-versed interpreter, of the metaphorical language typical of ancestral literature.
3. Know exhaustively, the fauna and flora of your country and the therapeutic and magical utility of a large number of plants.
4. Know the fundamental ideograms (Odù de Ifá) and the incantations inserted in them.
5. You must constantly raise your level of theological and scientific information.

"In Ifá there is not everything, in Ifá everything fits".

This serves as a universal data bank where all existing existential events are stored, classified in the Ifá code.

"The true way to know nothing is to want to learn everything at once"

Ògbè Òdí

SOME ESSENTIAL ELEMENTS FOR THE INTERPRETATION IN THE ACT OF DIVINATION.

Ká firè fún ----- Finish comforting.

A dífá fún ------ He was in search of divination. Lodá fún ------- You will perform the divination.

Mo firè fún ---- Òşà that we must take as a behavioral reference (her example or behavioral pattern in history or pataki that she refers to).

Abo fún -------- Who is close to the consulted.

Ajogún --------- Bad spiritualities (Death, illness, loss, etc.)

Ayanmó (Añamó) --- Destiny.

Áyewo (Ayeo)   Hex.

Ké fèrí lorí..........Incredulous.

Kán Kán lòní -------- Quickly, today, right now. Kí nnkan má şe ---- Protect from evil forces.

Kó le ni ó díwo (Koleniodio) --- It shouldn't be occupying you all the time. Jálè   Complete.

Mo jálè ---- Continue further.

Kòtó jálè --- It is insufficient, follow it or complete it.

Bé ko yes ---- Begging for something that is not there (is something missing?). Laarí işé òrìşà? ------ Is a job with Òşà important?

Ní torí, Intórí ------- Because of.

166

Lésè -------- At the foot of, follow the trail. Lówó ------- at the hands of.

Igbó -------- Forest, mone, manigua.

Ode..........Hunter.

Dáfá..........Divination.

SOME IRÉ E IBI (OSOBO) IMPORTANT

IRÉ

Iré aikú -------------------- Health benefit and long life

Iré àṣẹ́ gun ----------------- Benefit to win or conquer

Iré àṣẹ́ gun ọ̀tá ------------ Benefit from defeating enemies

Iré aya ---------------------- Profit from a wife

Iré deedeewántòloòkun -Benefit of coming and going to the sea, fishermen, merchants

Iré omaa --------------------Intelligence benefit

Iré ìrìnkiri (inikini) -------- Travel benefit

Iré lésè eegún ------------ Benefit at the foot of the dead

Iré lésè ẹléda ------------- Benefit at the foot of the creator

Iré mérin layé ------------- Benefit that comes from the four parts of the world

Iré nlọlé siwaju -----------Benefit of improving by going to another land

Iré nṣowó (Iré ṣowo) ---- Profit of doing business

OSOBO (IBI)

Afitibó --------- Unexpected death

Akóba --------- Unexpected punishment, an unforeseen evil

Àroye............Complaint

Àrùn (anu).......Disease

Ejo (eyo)...........Judgment

Ikú..............Death

Iyan (iña) ----- Hunger, famine, etc.

Òfo ------------- Irreconcilable loss, divorce, differences

Òràn (ona) ----Big problem

Ònà ------------ leather, bumps

169

ELEMENTS OF DIVINATION FOR COMMUNICATION WITH ORI (ÌBÒ)

Apadí (Akuadí) ---- Piece of porcelain slab, opposite to iré.

Apa (Akua) --------- Bull's-eye Seed (beat opponents).

Gúngún ------------- (death, deceased and conclude).

Igbin ----------------- Elongated snail (Ayé), means union.

Òtá ------------------ Small stone, longevity and war.

Owó ----------------- Double snail (cowries), currency, profit, acquire. Àwòran (Awona) --Small image of cloth or clay.

Àgbálùmò ----------.Caimito Seed, enjoy life

Efun ----------------- Cascarilla Ball, represents purity.

Eyin (eñi) ---------- Tooth of an animal, irreparable loss.

Isìn ------------------ Seed of the vegetable Cease, represents

Òrúnmìlà. Sáyò ----Guacalote seed, children and multiplicity of goods.

THREE ODÙ MAKE UP A "DETERMINING FIGURE OF IFÁ" WHEN THE ORACLE IS CONSULTED.

Considering that an event is given by a query that a person makes to the Ifá oracle. Three esoteric figures will be considered as a general rule, which from these events emerge to take into account:

The first reading is called: Odù Toyale Iwá (1680 stories; patakí; eses).

This Odù investigates and explains the destiny of the person and in turn represents their problems.

The second reading is called: Odù Okuta Kulá (1680 stories; patakí; eses).

This odù reaffirms in detail what is expressed in the Toyale, it speaks of the causes of the person's problem.

The third spread is called: Odù tomala belanşe (1680 stories; patakí; eses).

This odù reaffirms what was expressed by the previous ones and in turn provides various possible solutions to the person's problem.

There are also two others important odù to take into account: The Boyuto odù that is a kind of guardian odù of the Toyale odù and its writing results from the opposite writing of its encryption. And the odù Omotorun Iwa which is the odù formed by the union of the ends of the odù Toyale and the odù Tomala belanşe.

Each Odù is supposed to have 1680 of those stories related to him, and this along with those of the other odù, and each one of them is supposed to be known by the Bàbálawo who is the one who guesses and sacrifices, it is expected that he has it in memory, although we have not found any capable of that feat ......

Ifá Divination page 16 Willian Bascom (End of quote).

And we also find that some authors of works and writings specialized in these matters, agree with these criteria.

As each odù will have 1680 possible stories related to it, and with equal possibilities for all. Since the probabilities for the three odù are the same, that is; 256 times for each of the positions in a query to the Ifá oracle, that is: 256x256x256 = $(256)^3$ = 16, 777,216. (Sixteen million seven hundred seventy-seven thouSand two hundred sixteen). This means that there are the same possibilities for each event, if we divide 1 by the number of possibilities in the event, a figure will be so small that it tends to be considered or taken "as zero probability". It is evident that the result of this

172

mathematical operation tells us that it is very unlikely that this same Ifá figure will be repeated for many consecutive events, taking into account that, for a certain figure, there is an intrinsically concatenation of ideas. Expressed and summarized in the odù of Ifá. For these reasons it is practically impossible for any human mind to be able to store, keep in its memory and at the same time process such a volume of information in a minimum of time or duration of a consultation, so that the consultant can be considered optimal conditions and ready, to give an adequate response to each of the issues that you face when consulting the Ifá oracle. Unless, you use modern search and information processing methods that are very fast and efficient. Only Olódùmaré its creator and Òrúnmìlà its interpreter, are able to achieve it efficiently. I suppose that a human being would have to live around 700 years of life, with a brain in optimal conditions to be able to achieve it.

SOME EXPRESSIONS YORÙBÁ

Béẹ̀ ni.- Yes.

Béẹ̀ kó / ó ti.- No.

Ẹ̀ṣé.- thanks to you (to a superior or someone older than you).

Óṣe.- thank you (to someone younger than you).

Mo dupé.- I thank you.

To dupe.- We thank you.

Mo dupẹ́ pupò.- I thank you very much.

To dupẹ́ pupò.- We thank you very much.

Kò topic.- You are welcome / It is not mentioned / it is nothing.

Àlàáfíà.- Humbly greeting "be the Good", a way of greeting someone wishing them well at the same time.

Note: This greeting is best used between relatives or with people younger than you. It is not considered an acceptable greeting for an older person. In some cases, this may be the greetings used to greet and show respect to a priest of an Òrìsà, but when used in this way it is accompanied by a specific ritual gesture to distinguish it from a social greeting used between peers.

Ò dàbò.- Goodbye.

Note: This greeting is universally used among peers and is liked by the elderly.

Ẹ má bínú.- I'm sorry (to a superior or someone older than you).

Má bínú.- I am sorry (to a fellow man or someone younger than you).

Ẹ kò topic.- You are welcome / It is not mentioned / is nothing (to a superior or someone older than you).

Kò topic.- You are welcome / It is not mentioned / it is nothing (to a similar or someone younger than you).

¿Kí ni orúkọ rẹ.- What is your name?

Orúkọ mi ni.- My name is.

Note: It is generally considered improper to ask someone's name in Yoruba culture. The idea of introducing yourself greeting, but asking for your name is a concept of cultures foreign to the Yorùbá culture. The exception is when someone older than you ask for your name, this is considered acceptable.

Ẹ dide! - Get up (to a superior or someone older than you).

Ẹ jókòó.- Sit down (to a superior or someone older than you).

Dide! - Get up (to a peer or someone younger than you).

Jókòó.- Sit down (to a peer or someone younger than you).

Ẹ Madide! - Do not stand up (to a superior or someone older than you).

Ẹ má jókòó.- Do not feel (a superior or someone older than you).

Madide! - Do not stand up (to a peer or someone younger than you).

Má jókòó.- do not feel (like someone or someone younger than you).

Mo féràn rẹ.- I love him (a person, singular).

Mo féràn yin.- I love you (more than one person, plural).

Mo naa féràn rẹ.- I love him too (one person, singular).

Mo naa féràn yin.- (to more than one person, plural).

176

VOCABULARY USED

The list in the next section presents some forms commonly used in the Yorùbá language that are directly related to Òrìṣà or to the practice of Ifá.

Abo.- Female (indicates gender, does not speak of a woman).

Abòrìṣà.- A worshiper of the Òrìṣà, most often used in the Diaspora to signify someone who has received some basic initiations. This distinguishes that person from the rest of the community.

Àbọrú Àbọyè Àbọṣíṣẹ.- To be able to sacrifice / a prayer for the sacrifice to be heard To be able to sacrifice / a prayer for the sacrifice to be accepted To be able to sacrifice / a prayer for the sacrifice to manifest "Àbọrú, Àbọyè" is considered one of the appropriate greetings for a Babaláwo or Ìyánifá (initiated in Ifá). The priest will return the greeting of "Àbọṣíṣẹ." In many cases and the blessing will extend to the initiate return this greeting. This varies from priest to priest.

Àdìmú.- The food offered to the Ancestors and / or Òrìṣà.

Àdúrà.- Prayer.

Ako.- The male (indicates gender).

Àlàáfíà.- Greeting that means "be the Good", a way of greeting someone and wishing them well-being at the same time. See the important note below the greetings section.

Àşẹ.- The life force; a common meaning; "The power to manifest" or "is for what".

Awo.- The mystery; a name for all the devotees of Òrìşà; a name for an individual Òrìşà priest; a term that identifies the religion of Ifá.

Àyèwò.- Research, often used instead of "Ibi" in divination to indicate the need to investigate the problems further.

Baba / Baba my.- Father / my father.

Babalórìşá.- Male priest of Òrìşà, often the father of spiritual children.

Cuje.- It is a fine rod made from the branches of the tree ("Rasca Barrigas")

Ẹbọ.- The sacrifice to offer. This can be used to indicate the offering of blood to the Òrìşà although in the Diaspora this is often used as a term indicative of generally offering something to the Ancestors and the Òrìşà.

178

Éérìndínlógún.- The name of the sacred Oracle of the initiates of ìrìṣà.

It also refers to the sixteen cowries used during divination; the translation speaks "twenty minus four" which illustrates the Yorùbá way of calculating certain numbers.

Èèwò.- The taboo.

Ẹgbé.- Society or group of people, for example, Ẹgbẹ́ Ọ̀sun is a group of initiates of Ọ̀sun.

Èjè.- Blood.

Ẹmu opé.- The palm wine.

Epo Papua.- Red palm oil.

Ewé.- Leaves or herbs.

Ibi.- Bad luck, bad fortune.

Ìbọrì.- Ritually serve the head, praising and feeding one's Orí.

Idè.- The ankle bracelet, bracelet or necklace, refers to the sacred articles adorned with Òrìṣà beads, although it is more used in the Diaspora to indicate a bracelet of some kind.

Igbá.- Literally "the gourd", but it is often used to indicate a container filled with the sacred mysteries and the

179

consecrated instruments of the Òrìṣà example, Igbá Ọ̀sun is Ọ̀sun, the sacred ritual container.

Ikin Ifá.- The sacred palm nuts used in the most important divination rituals.

Ilé.- Accommodation, house, describes a family from Òrìṣà.

Ìlèkè.- Literally "the beads" but it is often used to refer to the sacred necklaces adorned with Òrìṣà beads.

I'll go.- Good fortune, good luck.

Ìyá, Ìyá my.- Mother, my mother.

Ìyálórìsà.- Priest woman of Òrìṣà, often the mother of spiritual children.

Obì abata.- The cola nut.

Obìrin.- Female or specifically a woman.

Odù Ifá.- The 256 signs or marks used in Ifá divination that represent the fundamental forces of creation in the universe, it is literally used as a reference to the body of Ifá.

Ọ̀gbèrì.- Someone who has not received any kind of initiation into the mysteries of Òrìṣà, a novice.

Ọkùnrin.- The male, specifically a man.

Olorisà.- An initiate of the Òrìṣà man or woman.

180

Sometimes this word is used to indicate someone who has been initiated into the mysteries of Òrìṣà but has not been spiritually initiated through the rites of consecration.

Olúwo.- In Ifá this term can be applied to an Ifá priest. The general meaning of the word indicates a person who teaches religion. It may, in some cases, indicate a certain line within the Ifá priesthood.

Omì tútù.- Fresh water

Omìèrò.- Water with consecrated herbs, "tranquilizing water".

Ọmọ.- The child, after spring. This can be used to refer to the biological years of spiritual children.

Ọ̀pèlè.- The Ifá divination chain.

Òrí.- White cocoa butter.

Oríkì.- Name of praise or story; sometimes used as an invocation to the matter of the Oríkì.

Orin.- The song.

Orógbó.- The bitter cola nut.

Ọṣẹ Dúdú / Ọṣẹ Aládin.- The black soap.

Ọtí.- A general word for spirits or wine.

Owó.- The money.

Oyin.- Honey.

SOME TERMS

Ajagún - The Yoruba term for warriors like the Orişa of protection.

Ajogún - The Yoruba term for denying forces.

Babalawo - The priest with a high degree of knowledge within the religious structure of Ifá.

Eegún - Hereditary entities.

Egúngún - The society within the Yoruba cultural structure that communes with and maintains the traditional directives of the ancestors.

Ehin Iwa - The Yoruba term for after life and reincarnation.

Elegun - Those initiated priests and priestesses who are possessed with the Orişa.

Enikeji - The Yoruba term for the guardian angel.

Eniyan Gidi - the Yoruba term for the authentic or true human being.

Idé - Sacred beads worn on the left wrist by Ifá devotees.

182

El llé-Ife - The ancient spiritual capital of the present Yoruba nation.

Ìmoyé - like wisdom

The Fá de Ìpìlé - The process of determining one's African origins, using the Ifá divination system.

Ìrùnmolè - The Yoruba term for divinities.

The Ìyáamí - A Yoruba term for witches (The Mothers).

The chestnut tree - The term applied to the societies of freedom established by the African captives escaped from the "New World". Technically, this word is Spanish and is used for sheep or cattle that have been lost.

Odù - The sacred text and the religious body of Ifá; that was named after the admired wife of Orunmila. Also, the term applied to the vessels containing the consecrated objects of the priests.

Odùdúwà - The patriarch of the current Yoruba nation that he established himself.

Ogbọní - The society of superiors within the present Yoruba cultural context, which maintains the connection with the Earth and the cultural forces of African society.

Olódùmarè - the Creator - God in the Yoruba cultural context.

O'lòrìṣà - The Beginning of the priest or priestess within the Yoruba religious structure.

Òrìṣà - The interpretation of Ifá, of energy forces that emanate from the Creator.

These evolutionary divinities are also declared anthropologically as cultural archetypes of light and avatars.

Òrúnmìlà - The prophet, established by the religious cult of Ifá.

ABOUT THE AUTHOR

Marcelo Madan born in 1944 in Santiago de Cuba. He comes from an Afro-Cuban family with deep religious roots. Consecrated in the orisha Obatalá since 1951. Awo of Orunmila, consecrated in Ifá as Babalawo by his godfather Ruben Pineda (Baba Ejiogbe), since 1992. His paternal grandfather, Eligio Madan "Ifanlá" of slave parents brought from Africa and a native of Jovellanos in the province of Matanzas Cuba.

His maternal grandmother María Belén Hernández, a famous Iyalorisha from the city of Havana and consecrated in the orisha Obatalá. His father Eligio Madan Hernández Awo de Orunmila (Ogbe Owonrin) and consecrated in the orisha Oshun. His maternal grandmother, a famous Iyalorisha from the city of Santiago de Cuba. At the beginning of the forties and fifties Rosa Torrez "Shangó Gumí", who together with the famous babalorisha also son of Shangó Rinerio Pérez, Amada Sánchez and Aurora La Mar el Oriate Liberato and others, initiate the first settlement of orishas in that city; She is the granddaughter of Ma Braulia, a free woman who came from Africa. Veneranda Constanten, her mother, also consecrated in Obatalá (Ewin fún), she dedicated her whole life to religious work together with her mother, Rosa Torrez.

These are the deep ancestral roots of Marcelo Madan, which allowed them, through his consecration from an early age, to acquire the knowledge to carry out his religious literary works. And since then, he has become one of the most important researchers of the "lukumises" religion in Cuba, publishing dozens of books, among which are: the "Treaties of Ifá, Synthesis of the odu of Ifá, Orish Collections, The Oracles of the Orishas, Pocket Manual for Santeros, Meals and Adimú for the Saints among others.